ENDORSEMENTS FOR "FOREVER HOPE"

To be successful in life is a hope shared with multitudes worldwide. In so many ways people portray this longing for success, they cheer on their favorite sports team, buy the T-shirt with their favorite's players name on the back and proudly wear it as they walk around town. The books that so often are best sellers are the books that outline the principles to success in life, whether it is to do with the business world or in Christian circles with principles of how to grow the church, people are looking for success. The problem and reality are that successful people are in the minority when it comes to receiving the accolades the world views as success. The real question we must ask is 'How does God view success?' When we search the scriptures we find the Lord honoring faithfulness, with what he has given to us, the exhortations of the writings of the Apostles are to understand that through all of life's difficulties to trust and believes that even in the most difficult times that God is still with us.

In this book 'Forever Hope' Donna takes us on a journey, her personal journey through life, and how she has kept faith in the midst of severe trials. When life throws a curve ball and suddenly everything changes, when grief becomes a daily battle and the world suddenly seems to lose its colors and appears grey. I think that is a little of what the Psalmist meant when he penned those well know words from Psalm 23 …'though I walk through the valley of the shadow of death I will fear no evil for You are with me…'

The good news is we don't stay in the valley we walk through it! As Donna shares her heart, her struggles and her faith, may you too discover the faith to walk through your valley into the glorious light of God's embrace and love. And one day hear the words that define real success 'Well done good and faithful servant'.

Pastor Keith Tipple
Author of 'The Gospel We Preach' and 'There Is Always a Way Back'
www.ocean-wings.net

Life is full of ups and downs ... some gentle, some dramatic. With words of faith and hope, Donna has captured the sense of a life well-lived and grounded in an unshakeable belief in God's greater plan for our good.

Christa Hutchins
Author of 'Moving Forward'
www.doanewthing.com

Forever
HOPE

Forever HOPE

Living in hope in the midst of life's struggles

DL Rudd

XULON PRESS ELITE

Xulon Press
2301 Lucien Way #415
Maitland, FL 32751
407.339.4217
www.xulonpress.com

© 2020 by DL Rudd

All rights reserved solely by the author. The author guarantees all contents are original and do not infringe upon the legal rights of any other person or work. No part of this book may be reproduced in any form without the permission of the author. The views expressed in this book are not necessarily those of the publisher.

Printed in the United States of America.

ISBN-13: 978-1-6305-0312-3

DEDICATION

This book is dedicated to the best sons a mom could ask for. You are the truest loves of my life, after Jesus Christ, who will always be my First Love. Christopher, Michael, Jonathan, and my daughter-in-love Elizabeth, you have filled my heart to an overflow that is as deep and wide as the ocean God created, for such a time as this.

To my baby boys, Bryan and Mark, who I held in my arms only a brief moment, although you never got to live your life to the fullest on this earth, you rejoice with your Dad, Auntie Liz and Omi, along with many other family and friends who have heavenly mansions with God.
I can only imagine how beautiful it is; you are dancing with Jesus.

Eternity awaits our arrival, and we will be together again. We will have no more hurt or sadness from this world.

Forever HOPE

I will carry on the message of Jesus Christ while I am here on earth and look forward to the day we are reunited again.

Written to an audience of One. Jesus, I love you. Thank you, Lord, for this very personal journey. Without you, I can do nothing.

TABLE OF CONTENTS

Endorsements i
Dedication. vii
Introduction. xi

Genesis 1
The Bonds of Sisterhood. 13
The Future Unfolds 23
Children are a Heritage. 41
The Future Stolen 105
Facing Goliath. 137
Living in Hope 151

Final Words. 161

INTRODUCTION

I treasure your time, as I share this personal portion of my life with you. I hope you sense that I am talking with you as a friend, while we sit on a porch swing sipping a cup of coffee on a comfortable breezy day. May you find hope in your journey, no matter the circumstances. God brings the rainbow after the storm. So, take a deep breath and soak in His truth and goodness.

Now grab your coffee cup — you might need a tissue, then— come join me in this journey called life.

More than thirty years ago, God began preparing this book, for this very time, through my person life events. It is written with prayer and anticipation you may be encouraged.

If you are not a Christ follower, may this story touch you in a profound way so you sense His freedom. Please pray the prayer of salvation at the end of the book, to live a life that leads to Eternity with Christ. He is real. He loves you, just as you are. So, one day, if we don't meet this side of Heaven, we will encounter each other in Heaven.

Forever HOPE

What sweet hope!
To life!
Abundantly living in Christ

I write this book to everyone who realizes that we all have struggles in our life. Hope is our gift from God. During tough times, no matter the circumstance, we need to be patient and learn from events that happen to us. Be prayerful as you walk through the deep dark roads you encounter. The light is indeed at the end of the tunnel. Hope is ours, grab it and never let it go.

Experiences we walk through, are sometimes easy, other times difficult. Each one offers a lesson if we are willing to discover the valuable messages within our mind and soul. God has the answers to the questions we ask. We need to appreciate that often times he doesn't give us the reasons why we have troubles, but we can still learn through our circumstances. This brings us wisdom and strength, especially when we lean on Him to guide us through the valleys and mountains.

An important factor when we walk through challenging situations is to bring any pain or hurt to the surface. Allow restoration to happen, because when we do, Jesus, who is Healer can begin to fill in the emptiness, sorrow and pain. He came to this earth to help us. We have biblical stories telling us what He did, so we can relate and live with His liberty.

Introduction

Yes, you too can live free; full of joy, love and grace. God says so repeatedly. Don't think he's given up on you. He never gave up on me. That's why I share this book with you.

The experiences I will share should have overwhelmed me. But God was in the midst. He never left me, never forgot me. He walked with me, sometimes he even had to carry me as I went through the valley of death, a few times.

Amid sadness and quite a few riptides; there were moments when I felt my life was in the center of a hurricane. God gave me strength to get through each storm. So, when the morning came, an unspeakable joy from the sweet heart of God filled me up, as it helped me walk into a new day. His mercy ran through my soul.

With some being deep and sorrowful events, God always brought me into a place of peace. The peace that only He can offer.

God's amazing devotion to me has been truly evident. He continues to shine his love over me every day. It is a treasured gift that I never want to take for granted.

With that said, there is no sugarcoating how tough life can be. It doesn't get easier, but it does get better. Wisdom is the gift that keeps on giving within the soul.

Not because of what I do, but what God does within me; he sees me though each scenario in life and stabilizes the craziness from trials that attempt to shake my world.

God gets *all* the glory. He loved me so much that he brought me out of a non-churched home, into His Kingdom. Unquestionably offering eternal life in Heaven when I asked him to forgive me of my sins. We are all born with this sin nature, which began in the Garden of Eden with Adam and Eve.

When we mature to the degree that we understand life is not about "me", it's about God and all he has done, we can walk out from the past, leave it behind and enter into a future filled with God's best.

What does best look like? Best is healing in our mind, body and soul. When we experience this, we can live in a place of peace and comfort, which offers freedom.

Are you ready?

Let's dig into some experiences that help teach these very treasured truths in

God's amazing love! Prepare yourself to hear from God. He will speak into your life as you read. No doubting. Simply believe.

GENESIS

The formation or origin of something.

*God knew the day I'd be born before I was in the womb.
He had plans for me to grow in Christ and share the
power of His love and grace.*

Walking up to the second floor of a newly built grade school seemed oddly strange, even for a fourth grader. The stairwell was lit well, plain, no bakery smell like I had experienced at the previous school I attended. It was October; the sun came through the high windows that felt almost prison-like.

Arriving at the top of the vestibule, being led by a staff member, I looked around at the gray cement floor and open darkness. It almost felt eerily sterile, like a hospital setting. There were only two classrooms to the left of us, the rest of the floor was open and bare, only offering the occasional pillar that would eventually encase more classrooms one day. Cold. Uncalculated. Which left me to feel even more distant; the school year was six weeks into its semester making me feel even more detached from this obligatory new life.

I don't remember why I was late for class that morning. It's possible we were detained in the office completing the registration paperwork; whatever the reason, I was not happy with this new school year that I was about to begin.

Once entered into the classroom, the teacher introduced me to my classmates. I felt alone and very much like an outsider before the day was underway. Why did we have to move to this godforsaken place, out in the boondock's, away from where I was comfortable, in my familiar surroundings? Sadness gripped my mind. I did not want to be at this school. And it appeared to be so bleak.

That was 1970. We moved twenty-five miles from the south side of Chicago to a quaint and fairly quiet suburb to live with my grandparents. The house was an old two-bedroom, one bath, with a surrounding acreage shared with the county and the railroad where freight trains came through regularly.

Our life wasn't impressive, in fact, most might say it was boring, especially in comparison to what I observed in suburbia, where lifestyles were much different and definitely a higher caliber than where we lived before this change transpired. Many classmates were active in programs and sports, in contrast to our stay—at—home family of eight, that chose to garden and watch television.

At recess one of my classmates introduced herself. Exuberantly asking me if I were a Christian. I froze momentarily, unsure how to respond. It was a phrase unfamiliar to me and I surely didn't want to come across as odd as I felt with the wrong response. I think I shook my head. I don't do well when I feel backed against the wall. My mind froze as I searched frantically for the correct answer. I don't recall the response I gave, but she continued on, explaining she was reading a great book titled *The Cross and the Switchblade* by David Wilkerson; she insisted on lending me the book. Great! I thought. This girl had no clue how difficult reading in our home was, with no quiet time in our small humble abode. I needed quiet to read, which rarely happened at our house. She was persistent that this was a must read. At some point, she lent me the book. It was a challenge for me to complete but found it to be an easy read; and it was an interesting and enjoyable storyline, which had a powerful point: leading people to salvation in Christ.

    She proceeded to introduce me to another girl whom she was friends with. This girl was slightly taller than me and had long blonde braids. She was about as thrilled as I was to be put in this most awkward position. Few words were shared; yet politeness was extended. Recess was over. Relief! I looked forward to getting back to my desk and ignore everyone around me. I just wanted to be invisible.

    The rest of the school year was a blur. I don't remember much except the two girls, one overly zealous to be my friend, and the other politely quiet. The latter didn't seem to like me much. I wasn't too bothered by that, since I was not happy about living in this oh so peculiar little town anyway. I wanted to go back to the "city".

While reading *Cross and the Switchblade*, I couldn't comprehend the appeal of this book. Unbeknownst to me, I would soon find out that the two new friendships made, were about to rock my world, leading me into a brand-new life in Christ. His plans were to use two girls and their families to welcome me with open arms into their lives. I didn't know at the time how much I needed this addition to my life. It was and is a blessing, as we are all not just friends, but family. The book was a tool in my hand to learn more about the power of Jesus' salvation, and how a person can walk in His strength in a very tangible way. God had a way of working out details in advance. Being that I didn't fit in so easy with the other classmates, God used these two willing girls, who loved Jesus, as did their families to help me learn about Him. My faith was about to grow.

In my young and very naïve mind, I didn't understand how God was working out plans for my life. The specifics were being arranged well in advance, of which I had no clue that my life had a purpose. Even in the difficult nine-year-old, life transforming transition, God was beginning to teach me what faith was all about. This began my solid foundation in Christ.

I was also learning that life is full of changes. Sometimes we acclimate quickly, other times a bit slower! In time, I adapted to this new life, and town, even though I felt like a foreigner in so many ways. I was resilient; with God's guidance he completed his work through me, from the inside out. Yet, with that said, I dealt with some insecurities throughout my childhood. It was seemingly little things, like not having cool new clothes. Then, being separated from other kids in the community, since we didn't live in a subdivision, it kept me feeling a bit isolated. To top it off, I didn't know what this Christian life was supposed to look like, nor was my family willing to invite this new lifestyle I was entering into. But God knew. He was building me up, as I was maturing.

The best part of the move, was that the braided blonde-haired girl, who ended up being my truest and bestest friend that I could ever have asked or hoped for. We were indeed sisters at heart, and always referred to each other as such. Opposites attract they say. In our case it was true. We were fashioned together at the core of our being. Her mom became not only my Spiritual Mom, but an adoptive mom who showed me a whole different life of unconditional love. A component that was welcomed into the depths of my heart.

Antonia was bold as a lion. Wise as an owl. Stylish as all get out, with a wild sense of humor and a voice like an angel. She was the first non-family person who loved me as I was and told me so often. She saw potential in me and often affirmed how significant I was. It was through her, I felt truly loved and accepted. God was teaching me, at this young age, how to walk with wise people. I took mental notes of healthy affirmations as well as spiritual teachings in those early years.

I became acclimated to this little town, but it took a few years. I appreciated my new friends and their families who became an extended support system. What a gift!

I attended church with them, yet my mom didn't understand the importance of this commitment, which didn't happen weekly for me, as it wasn't allowed. Attending church became a welcomed companion compared to my home life, where there was no privacy. These early years were so pivotal as I learned about God, it was not only satisfying to my soul, but like a sponge, the bible bacame an integral part of my life.

The challenges began, as the enemy of the soul quietly and subtly whispered into my heart and mind that I was doing something wrong, (because of the negative feedback at home, where Biblical principles weren't understood). The Holy Spirit was at work within me, and although my mom didn't know it, He was at work in her life too.

At eleven years old, I accepted Jesus as my Savior. Which was problematic, since talking about God at home was not acceptable. During the most precious, life-changing moments in my life, a time that was transforming, there was an underlying sense that I had done something reprehensible, choosing to become a Christian (which was a tactic of the enemy to defeat my walk with Christ); it took some time to tell my mom once I made the choice to walk this Christian lifestyle.

Yet, I was confident that the spiritual things were a deep part of my salvation, I loved God, and new he was good. Nothing could tear me away from this love.

Genesis

These apparent judgements placed upon me as a child brought on confusion, even condemnation. Since I couldn't speak about Christianity, I began to segment my life into categories when around people. This became a necessary response throughout my life, being cautious what I could and could not say, especially at home. Perplexing as it was, the negative impact this created in my child's mind became a roadblock. I found it hard to communicate when sharing ideas that others didn't agree with. This would bring a sense of condemnation with some backlash from adults. Then to push further the insecurities, unsure what acceptable responses should look like, I would simply not respond. My coping mechanisms were to compartmentalize. This was a life lesson for me. Listening became a friend; compassion would become a core part of my heart and mind.

Moving forward into Junior High I still felt like the odd one out because my life was so different from most everyone else's. Extracurricular activities were not an option. Guidance developing my talents and gifts were non-existent. But music was definitely an outlet I enjoyed. It was also accepted in our family, as we all enjoy various types of genres. This became my go to fun place. The records and portable player were valued possessions for me. Music is easy, relatable and it brought comfort as well as exercise when the dance moves began! Something about music has a common denominator with people, it's an enjoyable outlet.

The bible became invigorating to me, even in the early days of reading it. I was given a Catholic bible as a child, but the language put me to sleep when I read it.

The wording was so formal, yet I knew there was a need to learn God's word so I could grow as a Christ believer. I took small steps. Small chapters at a time. I listened when being taught at church what God's instructions meant. I soaked it in like a sponge.

When I found a version of the bible called *The Book*, I grabbed it; it was so easy to understand. This precious Book is marked up, pages curled over, and highlighted with many notes; it is more precious than gold or silver! I treasure it still today.

Through the years, God was my guide. He strengthened me as a child, I never had any temptations to get into trouble. I had a lot more responsibility than most kids. My mom remarried before the move. She had three more children, and with me being the oldest, I was a built-in babysitter. Mind you, I love children, and we have a fairly large extended family. I am the seventh oldest grandchild out of twenty-four. It was expected of me to be "the example". The pressure was for me to be mature, so I never got to be a "kid". This was normal for that era. Yet, it led me into a perfectionist and performance lifestyle.

This was my young life.

Genesis

Water from the Well

- The upbringings and surroundings we encounter as a child, (and even into our adulthood), becomes a training ground. Often, we react to situations in life in a positive or negative way. For instance, finding my love of music that was acceptable with no repercussions. Music brought joy, fun and laughter.
- What is your go-to when insecurities rise up within you?
- How are you loving your kids? Simply providing for them is a parental obligation.
- How are you filling their creative minds, or athletic abilities? Do they go along with what you suggest they do, to please you, or is it something they are gleaning from, in the midst of growing through the process? Find out what each child is uniquely gifted in. Set a firm foundation for them to grow and be challenged, as they find the talents God offers to each.
- Pray and watch for those God moments to share with children, they need love and encouragement.

Reach out to them, right where they are. Siblings each have their own special place within the family and should also be uniquely developed. Fill their souls with positive reinforcement, along with disciple to teach good boundaries.

- With care and gentle coaching, you are supporting a precious life to become who he/she is destined to become. Be prayerful and open to God's appointments as you teach and grow your children.
- Without a firm foundation, sometimes we fall short when pressure is on. That may not be a bad thing, so never beat yourself up about it, but learn from it. Life is about grace. You'd offer grace and help to those you love, be sure to give the same to yourself.
- What area do you default to as a comfort place, a safe haven? (mine was prayer and music).
- Where do you find peace?
- Communication for some can be difficult to express. How can you gain progress to share and encourage love and kindness, when someone is going through a challenge? How can this communication change the outcome of your relationship, especially if the person feels confronted or defiled when being challenged?
- Look for ways to help someone, a coworker, child, family member or neighbor, come out of their shell by sharing unconditional love. There is no greater love than when we help another person. It is as

Genesis

simple as a word of encouragement or a hug. Who can you encourage this week?
- Actively pray and read scripture. These are mighty weapons needed to grow and live as we await eternity's call.

THE BONDS OF SISTERHOOD

A strong foundation of a sister-friend that sticks closer than a brother, is a true gift

One of the blessings of sisterhood, is that we can be happy for each other, even when feelings of rejection creep into our mind.

Our inner circle of high school friends all went to prom, except me. I had fun with the girls as we laughed, giggled and enjoyed the nail painting, hair designing, and perfecting the dresses so everyone looked their absolute best for the occasion. But once they went on their way, I was left alone.

After a few moments of feeling sorry for myself, I shook the feelings of sadness off, and continued to imagine the fun they were having at the dance, then traveling to their dinner destination to enjoy a fabulous grown up meal. There was no animosity towards my friends, I was simply happy and knew they'd have a fabulous time.

Liz and I never had an ounce of jealousy towards each other. Which, truth be told, is an amazing (God) thing. So often the green—eyed monster creates havoc in friendships, often leading to great distain. But we understood that our different giftings balanced our friendship, so there was never competition between us. Love is never jealous. I was happy for her when she was blessed and vice versa. This was one of many special blessings we shared.

We had such fun together, often times with laughter over the silliest of things, (I'm talking belly laugh, hootin' and holler kind of merriment, where we'd burn off calories!). We made up our own nonsense words that we'd use throughout our conversations, which was often times hysterical. Antonia often joined in with funny stories and laughter which flowed even the more. Joy is contagious, which is one of the reasons I loved them so much.

Music of course was essential too. Singing in the car, dancing in the kitchen, blaring the stereo from the bedroom, all bring smiles to my face as I write this; such marvelous memories and fun times we had.

My first, and second vacation were with Liz and her parents. Our family never went on vacations, so, it was a huge opportunity to join them on a car trip to Daytona Beach. It brought so much excitement to me, that I can't express it to the fullest extent on paper. To say I was thrilled, is an understatement! It felt as if for the first time I was able to "live" a real life by going on this simple vacation to the beach. The challenge became how to persuade my mom (it took LOTS of coaxing) to give permission for me to go twelve hundred miles away. I believe my grandparents helped her to release some fears. I was after all, going with the family, not just silly girlfriends who might get into trouble, as often times teens might do. She finally said yes, after much coaxing! Spring break arrived, and we packed ourselves into the station wagon and drove to Florida. Eight track tapes at hand, and a lot of laughter along the way.

I fell in love with the ocean, sand and saltwater. The blue skies seemed to have been painted for my enjoyment. The experience was a sense a peace and energy all at the same time. I was invigorated by the warm spring breeze spent with my friend. Sadly, when I came home, I seemed to have morphed and grown from this wonderful experience, which created jealousy in my mom. The tension was tighter than a two-inch rubber band. The peace and fun withered away quickly. At sixteen, jealousy, especially from my mom, was not the healthiest of situations. I understood she was sad because she wasn't the one who offered this experience. But I wished that she would have been happy that I had the opportunity to go to Florida with good people who loved me as their own. In my mind, there was no competition, but an addition to my family. That's what love gives. It offers the acceptance and care which enhances our life, never takes away. My mom struggled with that well into my adulthood and couldn't communicate how it made her feel.

Of which I leaned more into Antonia (aka: Ma) and her Godly wisdom and love. It felt as if she understood more than my own mom did. So often, Ma would comment that she would adopt me, then Liz and I could be sisters. She loved me as I was and didn't try changing me. She prayed that I would grow and become more in who God created me to be. It's not to say my mom didn't want me to grow into the woman God had designed for me to be, she didn't have the biblical background to offer this security.

One of the best treasures I had was the ability to talk about life with Liz. Being able to share my heart as a teenager with someone who understood and had Godly wisdom to help me through the less than easy relationship my mom and I had, was so necessary. I watched other child and parent relationships drive them apart. So often when a parent doesn't understand the child, he or she drifts away, possibly driven into some less than stellar circumstances. But, when we have God in the midst of our life, we can trust Him to give us direction, as we seek restoration and a solid relationship.

Liz, Antonia and I prayed often for my mom. There were insecurities I believe she had to overcome. It was many years later when my mom found a sweet spot within the gospel music arena, she began seeking God in a very simple way. When my mom passed away from cancer, just a few years before the writing of this book, she accepted Jesus as her Savior, and now resides in heaven. What an answer to the many prayers we prayed.

The Bonds Of Sisterhood

Again, grateful for my praying friend(s) and their moms. God was faithful to do a behind the scene work within our family. He answered – when my mom was ready. God is so good. He patiently waits for us to run to him, and I am so grateful that my mom did just that. The emphasis on how important the relationship with my extended family, was such an integral part of my life. Heaven's reward is great, when we gather together as one family in Christ.

When graduation time arrived, it was another big transition. Liz was moving to Florida with her family. This was heart-wrenching for us; we had become the truest of sisters over the previous eight years. We were the "good girls" who stayed out of trouble. We loved Jesus and obeyed our parents, (isn't that a song?).

The basic way we kept in touch (the old-fashioned way), was by mail and phone calls. I love to write, Liz didn't. I'd call and leave a message, she rarely called back. This was something we laughed about over the years. The calls, when made, were few, as we didn't have unlimited minutes like today. This was the beginning of learning a new normal. Yet, with the many miles between us, we continued to stay close, and always, "forever sisters".

One of the last days before Liz left, I wrote her a letter, one of many to follow. This one included the lyrics to the movie soundtrack "To Sir with Love", which was so spot on, as if I had written it myself for Liz, as we were walking into our adult life. It still brings me to tears-all these years later. The song tells the story of how one person helps the other grow from being a child, into a strong adult who appreciates what the world has to offer, even after school days are long gone. The love and bond shared by two best friends must move forward to find the way each must travel. Heart pangs and sincere love runs deeper than most roots. What a treasure. What a gift. We never took that for granted.

Liz was the one who helped me to become strong from the inside out. God knew we had an amazing sisterhood bond like none other. I was not the same fourth grade little girl, who had no individualism to declare. I was growing into myself, a fearless young adult. Mighty. Able. With God at the center. And, I was overcoming what was supposed to suppress me.

A new normal began, without Liz nearby. This weighed heavy on my heart. She felt the same; we missed each other tremendously.

To express further the sisterhood we shared, almost like twins, ironically, we both "fell in love" with guys named Bill, (not the same Bill, but two different guys) during high school. They were our heartfelt first loves. The anguish of not having them as a forever companion, became a hurricane of sorts within our hearts and minds. Tears fell like rain when the relationships did not flourish. The dry ache that filled our hearts like a desert the size of the Sahara was painful. Yet, over time, we gradually adapted without our perspective Bills. Liz and I leaned on each other during this pivotal time in our lives. We understood each other. We encouraged each other, knowing that love would work itself out, somehow, someway. We didn't understand the bigger picture at the time.

Those days were so sweet and innocent. (In time, we met the intended men we were to marry. Our husbands were levelheaded, mature, good guys, men that balanced our naiveté. We learned and grew in our relationships with these men of valor. Valuing the sanctity of marriage, we stood up in each other's weddings, became the Godmother to each other's children). Our bond was tighter than most blood siblings. It was a true treasure to have this sisterhood. We gave God the glory for this gifted kinship.

While Liz settled into her Floridian life, I continued to wonder what my future was to look like. I needed a job, so, as fate would have it, my first job was in a kitchen, *with my mom*!

During that time, our mother—daughter relationship was very strained. We were two very different people. This made working together rather interesting and brought on challenges. The struggle was real.

Often, struggles stem from difficulties that one needs to master; my mom was no different. I had hoped and prayed she could live in the freedom that only Christ offers. It would have changed our relationship into something strong and positive. Yet that never happened. I did pray and ask God many times, what to do and how to function in a positive way with my mom. It wasn't always pretty, but God did a work in me, which helped me not to carry the burden to change her. Only He could do the inner work to give her wisdom and strength.

I realized during my fairly short tenure in the restaurant business, that I did not like the food industry as a "career".

I don't do well with early morning work hours, as I am a natural born night owl. I tried adapting, but my body just refused to do well at four a.m. wake up calls. It's funny now, but not so much back then! I'm not one that desires to spend time creating delicious cuisine, (but I sure do enjoy when someone else does the creating though!).

So, I continued seeking and wondering what my purpose was, and how to find it. In that quest, I took a leap of faith and moved to Florida. Liz's family had room for me to live with them while I attempted to plan my future.

Once settled in, I began the job search, which I anticipated to be fairly easy. It did not turn out that way. Disheartened after a few short weeks, the only opportunities were with restaurants or as a hotel maid. A double whammy for me. I felt like a fish out of water in Florida. What's a girl to do? I continued the attempt at figuring it out, a day at a time.

Water from the Well

- Like the seasons change, choices we make offer a lifetime of learning, if we adapt to it. Goals and purpose are important, but prayer is the ultimate answer to life's questions. We ask, then wait, and wait some more.
- Map out in a journal by writing what your likes and dislikes are. Do this each time there is a new life event. Trust God to be your helper, he will guide you, as long as you believe he will.
- How can change happen? What is the plan that is designed for you? Take a look at what you enjoy doing, your gifts, talents and abilities. What is God showing you as you are praying for direction? Walk it out a day at a time. Trust that when mistakes happen, they help to teach as a part of the lesson. God also sends people into our life. Never underestimate the value of close friendships *and* sandpaper people. Each are there to learn from.
- How many really know who they want to be by the age of eighteen? If you aren't sure, start by

eliminating as I did with what I did not find enjoyable. Fine tune by experimenting with jobs that may turn into the field you will flourish in. It's never too late for change! In fact, it's not our life design to become stagnant. If you are in the same field for forty or fifty years and you hate it, make a change! Look at Disney, and Ford, they persevered even when they were told they were not talented, can you imagine?! And the story of Colonel Sanders, was in his sixties when he became the fried chicken sensation we've come to know. Keep searching for your passion. When you find it, the acceleration will take place, and you'll find that happy zone and live strong as you share your life with the world!

- Who are your closest friends? We normally only have a few. Are they closer than a brother? That's true friendship. Seek people who will have your back when life gets rough, one who will stay with you through thick or thin. It's worth the effort and time investing into solid relationships. If your friend is easily angered or jealous, becomes bossy, they aren't a true friend; choose carefully who is in your inner circle.

THE FUTURE UNFOLDS

*Love happens as our heart is open to receive it
then share it*

Five months before moving to Florida, Brian and I met. Ironically, as life can be, his best friend, who happens to be my cousin introduced us. They become good buddies a few years earlier. I heard stories of the glaucoma he was born with, from my aunt and uncle. They spoke of his humor, great disposition, and how grounded he was, despite the multiple eye surgeries he had in his lifetime. It's safe to say, they loved him a lot.

My cousin and his parents must have been certain Brian and I would make the "perfect" couple. So, when his sister (also my cousin, of course) got married, Brian was his date so we would meet. It was cute and amusing, yet I wasn't on the lookout for a guy. With a chuckled "whatever", and because I love my cousin, I agreed to meet this guy.

Yeah me! I was excited to attend my first formal event, to play dress up and dance 'til the cows came home. My focus was to celebrate and have a good time.

I was unintentional about finding a future beau in Brian, (or anyone). I wanted to dance and have fun with family. Simple. No need to complicate the event with a set-up, especially if it didn't work out. Yet, I knew my cousin had good intentions.

The wedding day arrived. People gathered at the church; the anticipation was high as we were introduced. We looked at each other, to what I think was supposed to be love at first sight with fireworks going off. We said polite hellos and walked away to find seats. Ha! Looking back now, I imagine everyone dropped their chins to the ground while they shook their heads. I still chuckle as I write this. There was no "love at first site" moment, much to my family's chagrin.

There were no clanging gongs, neon lights, move over because another wedding is about to occur. No siree bob. I walked in wearing my best turquoise and black polyester disco outfit, ready to dance. He wore a corduroy suit, ready to drink and party to the rock-and-roll beat. Total opposites we were. I wondered, 'who were these people we both knew, introducing us as if we had any commonality'? Ha! No way would we make a good match. No chemistry, no connection.

Yet, out of obligation to "family", I gave him my number at the end of the night, one he did not even ask for (imagine that). He put it "in his pocket," but it dropped to the floor, supposedly by accident. He "thought" it went into the pocket of his jacket. Minutes later, I saw it on the floor and said sarcastically, "ya lose something, or purposed to not want this number?". He sheepishly took the paper with some humble pie. Mind you, the poor guy felt he was under a microscope, and was a tad bit paranoid because we were among my family. No pressure at all for him, as everyone was watching every move we made, or so it seemed, at least to Brian!

In my mind, this was a no-win situation. I would not fret about this becoming any kind of relationship: no bells ringing in my mind, nor ears! I was moving on without him. He seemed to come to the same conclusion as I.

Weeks passed by before he finally called me, at which time I was not home. My mom answered the call; they ended up talking for over forty-five minutes. Say what?? He was trying his best to impress my mom, as most do with the first encounter with parents of someone you hope to date. Well, he won that round with ease. During their conversation, he name dropped by telling her he attended Elvis' last Chicago concert only a few years earlier. To say that she loved Elvis is an understatement. So, Brian became a part of the inner circle. My mom was impressed.

What captivated my mom was his polite demeanor and engaging conversation. The icing on the cake became their common denominator, Elvis. Two months after the attempted set up at my cousin's wedding, we had our first date. Ultimately, it was tousled here and there. His schedule. My schedule. He had big issues with his car, of which I thought he was lying. I thought he was politely shrugging me off, but because of the friendship he had with my cousin, he didn't want to be ungrateful to the well-meant plans for us to become an item.

In the months that followed, we had extensive and meaningful conversations about life, family goals, and aspirations. We had many similarities after all. It was as if our hearts were bonded before we met. We began to develop a deep friendship; roots were being planted.

With both sets of parents being divorced, we were hesitant about marriage. We agreed that marriage was a forever commitment, and the D word (divorce) would never cross our mouths, no matter who we married, each other or someone else. We vowed to hold each other accountable for such.

During our courting time, I felt as if I were going through some growing pains, and changes needed to be made. Much to our disappointment, after dating only a few months, I moved to Florida, (mentioned in the last chapter). We discussed the move in depth, talking pros and cons. Desperately seeking Donna, I needed to know who I was, and to find my purpose. Moving seemed to be the best option. As for our becoming "a couple", the timing seemed continuously off in our relationship.

As I shared in the last chapter, it blessed me to stay with Liz and her mom. Once there though, I felt nomadic, and frozen. Nervous and afraid of what the future was to look like, it seemed I was walking into the unknown with no sense of clarity. I wondered how I would find my personal life map that included directions to show the way. The career path I was seeking continued to come up blank. Unobtrusive. Tentative. Exactly what the enemy (the devil) of my soul wanted. To live in a perplexed state of mind. This would keep me from fulfilling my God given destiny, or at least delay it. I had to learn to trust God, something new and foreign to me. Most people find "their own way". But as a Christ follower, we need to invite Him into the mix. He knows the time and purpose of each of our lives.

I was certain of one thing. Whatever I did would lead me down a path that would help me grow into who I was to become. The right people, and the right place at the right time. Even the wrong choices helped me learn what wasn't right for me.

As I deliberated what my life would look like, along with millions of thoughts that raced through my head, Brian was back in Illinois, hoping I'd soon fly home so we could be together–forever. Absence seemed to make the heart grow fonder. I needed to break old chains of the past to create a fresh start in a new place. The inner tension of what to do was taut, yet my hope stayed alive. Life would work out, somehow, someway. I was in search of doors to open, like in the Price is Right. Which door would offer the big prize to reveal my life's purpose?

Months before I moved, when I expressed the need to do so, Brian wasn't thrilled with the idea, yet he understood the circumstances and the necessity for me to cultivate my future. In the many conversations we had, I thought it was a good idea for him to move too. He desperately wanted to find his way and his identity. He was incredibly gifted when it came to music, wanting to be a producer. But his dad utterly discouraged the idea, stating it was not a "real" job. Therefore, the idea died, sadly never reaching the light of day. What a colossal mistake. It was a passion that was never fulfilled. The world was denied someone who had an amazing talent that could have touched many lives through musical recordings. He would have lived in such freedom, but words tore him down, his ideas remained undone. It always saddened me he never fulfilled his calling, one he quietly struggled with throughout his adult life.

With that said, together, we weighed many options of what to do for the future, whether together or separately. We'd conquer the world, nothing seemed impossible. Love can move mountains when walking life out cooperatively together. That was our outlook. Naïve? Maybe. Hopeful, absolutely!

The confidence to overcome any obstacle, past, present and future was a yearning deep inside my soul. Two are better than one, espeically when help is needed. Yet Brian was tentative to move all the way to Florida and make a fresh start. During my stay, he sent me notes and poems, always filled with musical stanzas. He even created a cassette tape (that was as techie as it was back in the day), full of love songs, to which he wrote out the lyrics to each song, highlighting and writing tender notes, expressing his love for me, (how romantic, right?). I loved it, fell for it; tears would flow, my heart missed him more each day.

The Future Unfolds

He expressed as we talked on the phone of the strength I had, not just to move away, but far-far away. I had ventured into new beginnings, even though it was unknown and scary. He'd speak of how fearless I was to make this change and cut the cord. Removing restraints of childhood which held me back, it was a pivotal move; he was watching and observing.

There were moments in our conversations, a twinge of envy, yet I heard support in his voice. I felt it. His support to let me be free, was of great value and validated who I was becoming. It was courageous for me to travel twelve hundred miles away to "find myself". When he spoke these words into my life, they might as well have been gold, set into my heart. This love was growing stronger, but not making much sense because of the distance between us.

It wasn't easy, and sometimes quite sad. It was the right thing to do, yet never seemed to be a courageous choice. But it was a powerful choice to make. Reflecting, I had encouraged him to find the stamina to move too. Make a new beginning. It would have boosted his confidence.

Sometimes we have to live life by taking difficult steps which help us overcome our fear. Step out of living frozen. Some call it trial and error. However stated, life can seem uncertain while we live it.

The foundational experience was being established for me, yet didn't understand it, in that moment of time. God was my companion, my source of strength and love. He gave me courage to live each day.

While missing each other, not knowing how or when we would be together again, we both yearned for a clear road map to help us find our way. Our hearts were heavy as we missed each other. But I felt a newfound freedom. I am certain I prayed simple prayers during that time. Though I don't remember what words I said, God's grace was with me. I began yearning to live in the fullness of what I knew was mine in Christ. I was learning how to walk in His guidance, which was a new concept as a young adult; Real life, AKA: adult life was not as easy as I had imagined. Very thankful for God's grace. With some guidance, I was making choices, letting go of the child within to live in the fullness of His joy.

God knew the struggles. Sometimes words can be too many. The One who knows me and created me was with me as life unfolded, a step at a time. His sage correction as each scene of life played out was most welcomed, even when I didn't understand it.

Phone calls were sparingly between Brian and I, since we didn't have unlimited plans back in the day. Our conversations were much too short. So much to say, but so many words left unsaid, for time's sake, and fighting back emotions, so not to cry. There was always a void when hanging the phone back onto the wall. Heart tugs were felt as deep as the ocean at my doorstep.

About a month had gone by, each conversation would end asking me to come home. My answer was always, no way could I move back into the much too small home, with eight people, no privacy and lack of communication skills. Life had to work itself out, moment by moment.

Eventually, with a lack of options, I made the choice to go home. Florida wasn't my cup of tea. It's a great vacation destination, but not where I wanted to settle down to live. Liz did her best to persuade me to stay. I was torn, that was for sure. The decision was so much more difficult than I ever imagined it could be. And, once again, God's grace covered me, and I knew I could progress through this choice and the timing, trusting it would work itself out.

Offering my deepest appreciation to my sweet Florida family, a piece of my heart was being pulled out slowly. The love and compassion we shared, was more than I could put into words. When there is such a deep emotional and spiritual bond, our relationship was so much closer than blood relatives. Liz and I remained as close as sisters throughout our adult life. The brief time living together became a part of our strong bond.

I packed my suitcases and headed back home. It was not an easy conclusion to make, because I understood enough at the ripe age of eighteen, that whatever decisions made would affect my future. I did my best to choose as wisely as I knew how in the moment.

During the time I spent in Florida, Brian and I spoke about our relationship and the possibility of marriage one day; uncertain of how that would transpire while residing so far away, we knew it was a strong likelihood we would be together again. While those discussions developed, Antonia, my wonderful spiritual guide, expressed, short and sweet, as only a mom would do, that we weren't spiritually "yoked", being from different denominations. Innocently shaking off her suggestion, I was certain he would come over with ease to my side and experience the same freedom I came to know in Christ. Ah, this woman prayed. She guided me; I did not fully understand the depth of her teaching. I had so much to learn, but God was at work, as He always is. Even amid my inexperienced mind of spiritual matters, I was an innocent babe in the forest. Walking into mistakes that were inevitable, learning as I grew into the woman I was becoming, I sought God's plan and direction; even when it was only miniscule. I would grow, learn and teach the Gospel of Christ, especially through experiences that happened to me personally.

I can look back now with confidence, and know that I was, without a doubt serious about Jesus. Nothing would ever tear me away from His love. I knew in my heart that Brian would see the truth of what I knew in regard to the Bible. Jesus was the lifeline to live in freedom, and I trusted God in as much that he would catch the wave and ride it with me.

Once home, Brian and I began talking more in-depth about marriage. We were hesitant to some extent, due to both sets of parents being divorced. My parents divorced when I was a year old, so I never experienced what family life was like. I remember thinking it was a different situation from other kids. I would ask my mom when daddy would live with us. What made that even more heartfelt, was that my parents were soul mates and truly loved each

The Future Unfolds

other. More reason for me to ask questions when I was a young child, why we couldn't live together as a family. I don't recall my mom's response, but it was enough for me to be satisfied in the moment.

They eventually both remarried other people. I was truly blessed through it all, because my parents and stepparents all got along very well. By the time I got to high school, I understood enough to know my parents could not live together, both being strong willed by nature. It was not ideal, and not the way God intended. Marriage, I had learned through my parent's experience, is something that not only involves love, but intentionally working together, which leads to growth within the relationship.

Brian's parents, on the other hand, divorced when he was an adult. It affected him in a different way. Possibly more distressing because he had grown up with both parents under one roof, something I never experienced. For him, it brought a type of sorrow because the unity was broken, and the family would no longer be whole.

Our normal was different and complex. As we talked about these very personal experiences, we came to understand that once love and the vow to be married occurred, it was for a lifetime.

It was a topic of great significance for us, mostly due to how it affects the children. We understood that firsthand, and from different vantage points, young or older, divorce offers an ache and rawness of which no one wins.

We both agreed, throughout our many conversations, vows agreed upon in marriage were written in cement. In fact, we made an agreement, and literally pinky swore to hold each other accountable, even if we eventually married someone else. We would put our spouse and children before anything; jobs, people and projects. This was our final word, it would never be an option, and removed from our vocabulary, forever.

We were mature enough to have learned that marriage takes focus, adaptability and unconditional love. Something that is fresh and new every day.

As we both walked into adulthood, the insecurities from childhood hiked with us; this was a common denominator we both carried. I didn't realize it at the time, but it was as a big as a boulder.

There was something deep inside me, like an egg that's shell was breaking. This incubator I lived in, as a child, would become something in my past. Once I moved to Florida, I realized the inner strength to change and do things out of my comfort zone. It would be liberating as hope was growing a deep foundation within me. Also, I realized the freedom in God that was taking flight in my soul. With Him I could overcome all obstacles in life. I was certain Brian would break out of his shell too. He had so much to offer the world. But he had to find his inner strength, one he never got a hold of.

It was almost too uncomfortable to watch. Born with glaucoma, and numerous surgeries due to that disease, made his eye scar up and look abnormal. Also, being born with a fairly severe port wine stain on half his body, kept him feeling less than whole. Which should not have. But he was often made fun of, stared at by people who murmured behind his back. I can only imagine how that became a barrier of insecurity.

Another big encounter that occurred, which hindered his spiritual walk with God, was when we got married. We chose to marry at the church we met, for my cousin's ceremony. As we attended premarital classes, it was important to my husband for his pastor to be involved in the ceremony. He set up an appointment to meet with him. As we walked into the church that fateful afternoon, we stood in the vestibule (not even in his office), to be told that if I did not covert, we could not attend church, and we would go to hell, because God only accepts those from that particular denomination. As you might imagine, that did not float well with me. Brian felt beat down, yet again. He didn't understand the complexity of how denominational barriers work. This was a big hurt for him. He did love God. But now, confusion set in, (which is an attack from the devil himself, who only comes to steal our peace, kill our spirit and destroy our faith, anyway he can).

Although dialogues about God, heaven, Jesus and the Bible, transpired, over the years before we married, he was restless and unsettled with his Christian walk after that moment; consequently, we had many conversations about Christianity over the years that followed our wedding day. It left him with doubt, and a plethora of questions.

I found out how unequal we were in our faith. Without a Biblical foundation in marriage, it's like living with a log sticking out a window. Cracks and leaks appear. We were divided like oil and water; we didn't need to be a vinaigrette which separates, but more like a heavy milk-based dressing, blended together well.

After we got married, Brian never felt he could go to church, take communion, nor was he "allowed" to read the bible. But he was watching me. I went to church faithfully each week. I read my bible, wrote many notes and I continued to learn and grow in Christ.

He never said as much, but he wanted to attend church. He knew taking communion was important. But he was told he couldn't. Due to man-made rules by a denomination. It's super important to know, there's no mention in the bible of denominations, which are rules and guidelines created by men.

We grew up in what we were taught. Neither of us understood the preparation needed to fight battles in life, which were to be in prayer and the Bible. We simply didn't understand how to do that during those early years.

This is where one of our biggest struggles began. I lived in God's freedom and learned scripture and His promises. Brian didn't live in the freedom God offered through his adult life. I prayed often that he'd lean on Jesus, who heals our pain and brokenness, and is the only One to offer Salvation to anyone who asks Him.

My heart went out to his aching soul, wanting desperately for him to live unhindered from the burdens he had; the inner battle was real, although outwardly he never dealt with it, God was at work within his heart; it just took a long many years to come to fruition.

Letting go of the past was the best part of cultivating the future. Healing was taking place, a little at a time. Joy, peace, and love continued to grow within my soul. I was certain my husband would join me on this journey.

It's important to understand, then and now, that our walk with Christ is never to be taken lightly. Trusting that God's Word never changes. He redeems. He did. He does, and always will.

Forever HOPE

Water from the Well

- The church is not about a denomination, (which are man-made rules), it's not a building, but the people who are followers of Christ. Christians walk in the Holy Spirit, with the Bible as The Guide. When Christ is the Savior of your life, salvation is real, through the bloodshed at Calvary.
- Important keys to growing in Christ:
  - Read the Bible regularly. It is through His Word, that guides our life with love and grace through Christ.
  - Encircle yourself with other believers who are Biblically based. These relationships help us with accountability. No man is an island.
  - It is imperative to have a firm foundation in Christ. He brings life.
- Prayer is very important. Daily talking to God, in your own words, from your heart is what matters. Talk to Him as you would talk to a friend.
- Find and follow through with the passions and gifts you have been blessed with. These are part of your

The Future Unfolds

personal life; use it in your vocation. It's not just a dream, it's a part of your destiny.
- Create timelines and goals with God's guidance. Listen for his still small voice to direct where you should go. Never let anyone talk you out of your dreams and vision for your life.
- When it comes to marriage, be prayerful and thoughtful of who you want to marry. Journal your hopes and dreams, asking God for the qualities in a mate which you desire. But.... hold loosely to those desires, the one you might think is "the one" could be detrimental to your life.
- In your seeking and waiting, be open to wait and wait some more. There may be a good reason for the delay. God knows the right timing. He's really good at answering your deepest desires and provides confirmation to you, at the perfect time.
- **Extra loving note:** When going into marriage, while dating, during the engagement, be in prayer. Seek God's plan. Be patient; search scriptures on relationships and meditate on it. Worship Him and take communion together, and He will offer you divine direction on the paths to take. Then when walking into the season of marriage, be prepared for bumps and bruises along the way, keeping communication open and share your lives together as one. Love conquers all.

CHILDREN ARE A HERITAGE

Children are a wonderful gift that God gives to bring much happiness

One of my biggest desires was to have an older brother. The idea of it was just too cool, as he would look out for my best, and guide me as a big brother should. I imagined him being a protector, a safety net and someone bigger and stronger that I would learn from; he'd be a loyal companion. This girl had her dreams!

But history made me the only child of my parents. It was a blessing, and knowingly, there are advantages and disadvantages to whatever the family size. I learned it was okay to be the only child of my parents, for many reasons, of which I won't expound on here, for times' sake. God added siblings when my parents remarried. I was much older, which made me feel more like a mini mom.

Forever HOPE

I'd always hoped for my first-born child to be a boy. It was one of those silent prayers God would answer. In fact, we ended up having all sons. There would be no dress up fun girl experiences in our family. Life was just as it should be with a house filled with guys.

My pregnancies were easy, from beginning to end, no morning sickness, only basic tiredness, and the natural uncomfortableness of bloating from a growing baby within.

I have three sons, who are wonderful, and the absolute loves of my life. But five sons were given to us, as gifts. Children are to be held, not with tight fists, but with arms and hands opened wide. God gives, Satan steals.

Our first pregnancy went well. Delivery day came. Our baby was ready to enter the world. I was hooked up to the many annoying monitors attached which made movement restrictive and obtrusive, but necessary.

Contractions were slow and inconsistent, which aided to the uncertainty of what I had imagined and learned from Lamaze class.

Across the hall, a woman screamed, who, for over an hour, bellowed: "Just kill me now, I can't stand the pain". Repeatedly.

Annoyingly frightened, I regretted not sticking to my original plan of adopting or becoming a foster parent.

A nurse came in to check on me after about fifteen minutes of listening to the screaming crazy lady. She sensed my trepidation, only to explain, "Oh honey, she's already had a few kids. She does this every time. It's not that bad". Tapping my leg, she assured me I'd be fine. Hmmmmm.

Children Are A Heritage

I wasn't convinced, as she walked out of the room. Why would anyone go through delivery more than once if it was THAT painful?

This being my first child, I went through the Braxton Hicks contractions before the final call to admittance into the hospital. The feeling of those "fake" or preliminary contractions felt so real. I wondered how bad it would be when the real labor pains began. Based on the screams from the woman across the hall, I was apprehensive.

Admitted into a room with no view at the end of the hallway, I was prepped and ready to go with the delightful contraptions that are supposed to guide us safely through labor.

Contractions were inconsistent; I wondered if we should have gone home. But the due date was on target, so we stayed. We waited. And we waited. Slow as molasses is what it felt like. My doctor was delivering other babies, so an intern came in one time to check on me. The nurses came in a few times but seemed bored with the duty, since nothing was happening fast; we appeared to be the forgotten ones at the end of the hall.

It seems as if the hollering lady took up all the nurse's time and energy. I must have been second fiddle since I was not the high-pitched demanding one, seeking the attention of the staff. The thought crossed my mind, maybe I should become assertively loud. I don't recall how many hours we sat in the room. It seemed like "forever"; no one was checking on us. Bored....so bored, even the TV wasn't interesting. We waited.

The hallway became quiet, as the brassy lady must have finally delivered her baby, ridding her of all agony. Soon after, stillness set in; something wasn't right.

A few minutes went by before my husband spoke up, asking me if the monitor stopped, or did it become unhooked? Since the machine was set up behind me, I couldn't watch it, but for assurance, I pushed the alert button to the nurse's station. No one responded. Brian proceeded down the to the nurse's station for help and expressed our concern. I wondered if it was first mom syndrome, to which the nurses weren't attentive, since labor was taking its time setting in. The staff didn't appear too concerned about me, as they moseyed in to check my status.

A rather tall nurse walked in, with the look as if I had bothered her by seeking assistance. She had no words or reply to our call as she approached my bed, even though Brian expressed to the nurses he felt ill at ease and asked someone come to my room. As she approached the machine, a sense of urgency fell into the atmosphere. She immediately left. Returning momentarily with the intern, who tried to act cool as a cucumber, he checked my belly, the machine, and replied as he put his hand on me, that we would go to the labor room and check things out further. My heart sank. I didn't know what to ask. Again, a hush fell into this space and time.

[Note of importance: I recognized something was wrong. Intuition. I learned from this experience to live by the inner nudge, which is a sign that something is offbeat.

Let no one boo hoo you or ignore you when you are certain something is amiss.]

The next few hours were a blur, as I remember little of the details now. My doctor came into the labor room, explaining the results found, were that the baby had died due to the umbilical cord around the neck. They could do nothing at that point to save him.

I regret not journaling during this time; it would have been helpful to have written down my thoughts to process while grieving and to recall the small details amid this catastrophic event. I suppose at the time, it was not a memory I wanted to keep on paper; it was too arduous as I desperately desired to move on with life and act as if none of this was happening. Simply wish it away.

At that point, I was induced to help aid the delivery naturally, since my body was reacting to the death by not going into labor on its own. Somehow the inner turmoil within played with my mind, wondering what I had done wrong to make this happen. I was crushed.

Hours went by, Baby Boy was not willing to come out. Medicines were given, I don't remember which ones, but I do remember wanting to go home to be alone; exhaustion was setting in and sleep called my name. The nurses were avoidant, understandably so. Brian didn't know what to do. He ever so gently expressed that he'd leave to make a few phone calls, (we didn't have cell phones then, so using the pay phone in the waiting room was the only option). He called his parents and mine, letting them know what was transpiring. They in turn would update family members.

Forever **HOPE**

Upset and concerned, this was rocking everyone's world. Compassion set in from our family and friends, as the very slow labor continued to go into the midnight hour.

I desperately longed for sleep, Brian was also tired, yet never complained as he sat by my side. Even in my state of fatigue, I felt bad for him. I was closing in on no sleep at the twenty-four-hour mark, as nurses quietly check on us. This would not be an average delivery. This was incredibly heart wrenching for all involved. Words were too difficult to express the natural way, silence was offered from the staff, along with empathy.

This was the section of the hospital that brought life, and here was death, knocking at the door. I felt helpless. Broken. The enemy taunted my mind and heart. Morning came again, with no baby born.

One of the head nurses came in for her shift to find me still waiting to deliver from her previous shift the day before. She was livid! And told the night nurses as such. She came with determination, care and confidence, expressing we had to get the baby out before my body turned toxic. She would have scared me if I weren't so weary. I expressed as much. She gave me a hug and made demands of things needed to deliver the baby, ASAP. She told me she was going to stay with me until the baby was born. No matter how long it took. She was an angel blessing on earth. I needed her wisdom and strength at that moment.

With much effort, pushing the baby out with no full contractions (we wanted to avoid a C-Section), a few hours later, our first baby was born. Lifeless. Beautiful. Every

Children Are A Heritage

part of him was perfect, no malformations at all. He was my clone. It seemed like I was looking at my very own baby picture.

I was moved to a private room, while they prepared baby Bryan. It gave Brian and me time to grasp the whole scenario, birth to death in one nanosecond. How to wrap around our mind around this was exasperatingly wretched for us, the staff, and our doctors whose sole desire is to bring sweet life into the world.

As the doctors, interns and nurses checked on us, in a timely but polite manner, as to not overload us with too much activity, it gave us time to react, so, if need be, they could call counselors in, as they would with any catastrophic event. Personally, I take difficult circumstances and keep them within myself. I soak in the quietness, gather my thoughts and from my heart, pray and talk to God, as I break it all down in my head, to process in my mind how to deal with it and overcome whatever the problem is at hand. It's just how I am wired. Everyone is different. Brian was there, that was all I needed. I didn't want swarms of people doting and talking endlessly. We sat in silence. Saying few words here and there when something would come to mind. Tears flowed from our eyes, as our hearts ached at the loss and the void, knowing we would not take our baby home to his Disney nursery.

Questions to God were asked in silence during those long moments. Writing this now, takes me back to that place. I can feel the sensory in that holding space, the grayness of

Forever HOPE

death and the quiet questions which whirled around in our heads and hearts.

A nurse came in and gently asked if I wanted to hold the baby. My mind wanted to snap. Of course, I want to see my baby. He's *my baby*. I carried him and just had the most grueling delivery; what kind of question was that, I transiently contemplated!? Under the circumstances, my mind was rational. I knew the flip side; a different woman may not have wanted to hold him. It may have pushed her over the edge holding a lifeless baby. I couldn't *not* hold him. I softly nodded, saying yes, bring him in.

I had to see his face. Hold him on this earth, if only for this one time. He was mine. He was Brian's. We loved him, even though we wouldn't see him grow into adulthood. Life can be revolting at moments like this. We needed to have closure. To grasp and know. To touch and feel. It would make it all real and bring closure. In those few brief and precious moments, we needed to hug our baby.

Wrapped up snug in a hospital blanket, there was my little man. The nurse tenderly and graciously held our baby close to her, as if it were her own child. She handed him to me, quietly offering help if I needed it, then discretely left the room, so we would have alone time with him. That touched my heart, and my mind, during this crazy unforeseen, unsolicited monumental life given, life taken away moment.

As I stared down into the beautifully formed blanket wrapped body, he had thin dark brown hair. A face that was surprisingly a replica of my new-born baby picture taken the day I was born. My heart felt like it froze and was being stabbed with an ice pick, the similarity took my breath away, as I stared into his little face. He was absolutely perfect. Sweet baby that he was, would never crawl, walk, potty-train, graduate nor have a family. Silence continued to grip the room. Words were too difficult to speak. Tears dropped, only a few, as if we wanted to hold them in, as a coping mechanism.

I held him, which felt like only a nano-second in time, as a thief in the night would sneak in and steal the treasure of my heart, I wondered if I had the option to never give him back; could the world stop circling, so I could hold on to my baby for a lifetime? Might that be a possibility? Could the pain disappear? It girdled my mind with too many words left unexpressed because nothing would change the situation. I held a lifeless baby in my arms, like a doll. We silently cried. My heart was hurting, but so very firm in knowing, that even at that moment, I sensed the nearness of God. Staring into this baby's face, he felt more like a doll than a newborn. Thoughts filled my mind like the swirl of a jet pool. I never imagined I could sense the powerful love of God, especially at that moment. He was real. The Holy Spirit was in the room with us, comforting our breaking hearts. In my deepest darkest hour, God's embrace was present within me, as I held our sweet little baby.

Holding him carefully, whispers were spoken from my heart to God's heart, as if it were only Him and me in the room. The unspoken words were direct, as I rededicated my life to Him. I remember the prayer very clearly, just as if I

Forever **HOPE**

said it to Him today: *Lord, I do not understand this at all. I am not happy with this situation. But you are the Creator of all things. This child, he is yours. I will trust you, and dedicate my life to you, forever.* Those tender words, in that instant in time, shaped the woman I was about to become.

I was not living this life out in my own strength; but God within me that offered comfort, knowing I would make it through this death, with a deepened faith. God was teaching me about life in the real world.

I meant every word of that prayer. Even though, at eleven, I gave my heart and life to Jesus. As an adult, it seemed to be at the depth of despair, God connected in a profound way, while I held this precious baby. Without doubt nor hesitation, I sensed a soothing peace enter our-room. Something detected when you know God personally, because he is so very real. The power of Jesus began the healing process, while grief was at the doorstep of my heart and mind.

The panged emotions were raw, like a lion eating flesh from his prey. Yet still in a tranquilly peculiar way, as my twenty-one-year-old mind went to God, my heart ached for answers. In heaven we know the lion will lie with the lamb, peace will be there, and all questions will be answered, in a matter of seconds. This is how it felt that instant of time. This lioness momma's heart connected with her precious little lamb, as I trusted the Lion of Judah, to be the keeper of my first-born son. Peace flooded my thought life. Words were few; the numbing echo of void-ness which words could not express the deep sense of loss.

In those brief moments, as I was seeking assurance, Brian mentioned that we would have to pray the baby out of purgatory. As I lay there with many thoughts running through my head, I was trying to comprehend the statement he made. My neck and head must have twisted around like a doll being swung by the hair. I am certain I had the crazy raised eyebrow with a fierce fire of squinted eyes as I gazed at this man, I called husband with unbelief and confusion.

Purgatory – what?!?! I sternly asked what he was talking about. He quizzically answered, being he wondered how I did not know what purgatory was. He explained it to me. I retorted, there is no such thing as our dead baby residing in limbo! It's either heaven or hell….in fact, purgatory would be right here on earth. The definition of purgatory is hell, limbo, despair, suffering, torment, torture, which sounds like earth and hell mixed together. He was silenced. Sadness came over his face with a ray of hope as he contemplated, absorbing my response. He was desperately desiring the assurance that our baby would not suffer but ascend to heaven.

I shared scripture truths behind my statement and strong belief, best I could in that exhaustive moment. Expressing with utmost confidence, this baby of ours is, without a doubt, in the arms of Jesus! Explaining to him, with the simplicity of Jesus communicating to us to bring the little children to him in Matthew 19:14, Matthew 18:3, Mark 10:13-15 and Luke 19:15-16; this is the firm foundation I was certain of, with an absolute assurance that our baby was not in such a place called purgatory. There was no waiting period for him. Here and now, and at that moment, this treasured baby was safe and sound, securely in Jesus' arms.

Confusion is a game Satan plays. This was one of those times for my husband. I hoped to clear that up with the biblical confidence I knew to be true.

When he initially made the statement, I answered him with a question. Would a good God, the One we believe in, and love, serve and lift in praise, be so cruel, as to send our baby to hell or "limbo" to be tormented and suffer, because he died before birth? God is a gracious God. The fact that our baby died before reaching the airwaves into this earthly realm, there was no waiting period. Never. Not for any baby.

What he understood was that it became our responsibility to pay the price for the dead, for an indefinite period of time. Can you see me shaking my head right now? I am.

Absolutely NEVER, was my response, as we conversed. Jesus already paid the price for our life at Calvary. No more sacrifice needed. We don't pray for the dead; we pray for those who are still living, who need to accept Jesus as their Savior. Scripture tells us, to be absent from the body, is to be present with the Lord. (2 Corinthians 5:8).

Beam us up Jesus! This happens instantaneously. Solomon says the human spirit returns to God, not to some place of punishment. (Ecclesiastes 12:7, Job 32:8). God preserves the spirit until He can return it in the resurrection from the dead when eternal judgement (either life/heaven or death/hell) is determined. (Ezekiel 37:1-14; Revelation 20:14-15, 21:6-8).

Children Are A Heritage

Without a shadow of doubt, I knew, in that moment of death, our baby was in heaven, yet Brian was not convinced. He spent years after Baby Bryan was born, ill at peace, from what he was taught. The teachings of what he understood to be truth, I knew had to be broken off from his thought process. I refused to allow those chains that bind and confuse to be weapons of discouragement to my husband's mind. This was a ploy from the enemy of the soul; I would not, nor could not watch him live life wrenched with the guilt and pain from this situation, which is what he lived with much of his adult life. He watched me, while my confidence grew stronger, even after burying our baby. I did not waiver in my belief in God. He saw the spiritual security I lived with, step by step, closer to God. It wasn't a denominational thing. It was and is a God divine moment which offered me peace. Something Brian wanted, but didn't know how to obtain.

It also troubled Brian, wondering if the baby would make it to heaven because he died before we could baptize him. The concern was deep, so deep, I sensed a brokenness about him that our baby didn't have the opportunity to make it to heaven.

While I laid in bed, fatigued from the long delivery, with a clear mind, I expressed to my husband that as soon as the baby died, he went to heaven. Explaining again that the bible clearly states Jesus calls the children to him. He wants those who have a childlike faith to come to him, and he accepts them without question, nor hesitation. Jesus is all about relationship.

We talked on that subject for years after leaving the hospital that day. God, who created this child, would not allow him to go to hell because he died in utero and didn't get baptized. That would mean God is a tough and bad God. He'd be unholy, unrighteous and utterly cruel. Which he is not. God is a loving god. Satan works in a way to harm us and bring our minds to not believing God. Eternity is secure when we have Jesus as our Savior. No doubts, no fears. Life is settled, by the blood of Jesus, which included our precious baby boy.

I watched my husband struggle with the thought of our baby not entering into heaven. It laid heavy on his heart. I explained God's Word the best I knew how and prayed fervently for him to recognize God's truth and love. I trusted God to give Brian a peace, so his heart and mind would be confident of eternity for our family as a whole. Praying became my first response. Prayer shouldn't be an afterthought, it should be the first action taken, especially when we run out of words. God knows the heart of a person. He knows how to help us overcome any circumstance or thought. I was learning to lean on Him. It's not always easy. I didn't take any joy in watching the stinging stabs of the devil's lies that played havoc in my husband's heart. I don't wish for anyone to live in a stronghold of any type! Prayer changes things. It is the most effective action we can take!

As I lay in the hospital bed, the phone rang. It was my dad calling to let us know that he contacted local funeral homes seeking information to arrange the memorial service for our baby. He confirmed with me what the process would look like, then asked for the green light to proceed with arrangements. It was an out of body experience, as I lay in the hospital bed talking to my dad about funeral details...... for our baby. We would meet at the cemetery, have a few words together as a family. Seamlessly, it all came together, a funeral was planned.

God's promises, as difficult as life may be for those who love Him, must realize that all things will work out for our good. This was my foundation to help me walk through this burial.

Kingdom work was being accomplished. We didn't understand the depth of how God was working.... until years later. Angels surrounded my family, with harp and lyre, bringing such a simple peace. His will, not ours. Our baby would be waiting in heaven for us one day. Backward as it seemed, it held a hope, that one day we'd be together, whole, with our sweet child, in Heaven. What a reunion that will be! The yearning for heaven became relevant. Although we still had a lot of life to live while on this earth, the promise of eternity was and is a reality.

As odd and uncomfortable as the funeral plans were to hear, the silence in our little room was deafening. Words were hard to speak. Disbelief settled in a bit deeper as we tried wrapping our minds around how this would affect our future. It took time. How would we get through a cemetery visit to lay our baby "to rest"? Through this experience, God gave me a peace that is beyond what I could imagine, just as he promises in the Bible. The pain was real. But God was bigger than what we were going through. We had to decide to live in a place of peace, otherwise, we'd be among the living dead.

It felt like forever as we waited to be discharged after giving birth. The doctors were kind enough, and with wisdom, knew I needed to go home to be in my own environment, away from other moms and their babies. I desperately needed my private space, to unwind and find a new normal. It seemed to take a lifetime for release papers to be completed.

The days leading up to the burial were a blur. The mind seemed to shut down as we walked through the emerging struggle. It was quite immobilizing, even as strong as I am. We drove fifty minutes to the cemetery with our parents and a pastor who was a personal friend. I don't remember much at all of that solemn day, other than simple prayers prayed. Silence and gentle hugs were shared between us. Yet still, I do remember being grateful for our pastor, who cared about our family, and all we were going through. It was a personal touch that brought great comfort. God was in every detail, making it easy to praise Him for the consolation and how the Holy Spirit brought peace in spite of the dark hole that we endured for the moment.

Once home, Brian and I did our best to walk into the future. Unclear what lay ahead emotionally, we conquered, with Christ, who captured our many tears and filled us up with more peace than we could have hoped for. We didn't become a statistic of our circumstance but lived through it. One step at a time, walking out, day by day. As healing

Children Are A Heritage

transpired, whole came into our lives. God's goodness was evident.

I was excited when we got pregnant again. Two years later, another boy was gifted to us. The fulfillment of my dream was coming true. Christopher was our sweet gift as our family grew. God was filling our desires. Love was growing deeper for all of us. This child was the absolute purest gift that God could have blessed us with. Never would he replace Bryan. But God gave us the gift of another baby.

This blond-haired blue-eyed baby was content and impeccable. Thank you, Lord, for such a wonderful gift in our Christopher. We were eternally grateful that he was easy-going, and so very happy all the time. Days flew by, as we enjoyed this content child. We learned to take nothing for granted.

Christopher adapted to a schedule with ease; he slept, woke, ate, played, smiled and slept again. He was simply delightful. A year flew by, and found once again, we were pregnant. All went accordingly, until a few months into the pregnancy when I began to spot small amounts of blood. Ok, I thought to myself, I'm not going to freak out or worry. Yet, it continued over the next few days.

I contacted the OB/GYN's office; we set a checkup date. Our doctors were the best around. They offered tender loving care, especially after the stillbirth of our first baby. They went above and beyond the call of duty with each of our pregnancies.

Appointment day came, the doctor checked and prodded as needed. With the humbling, uncomfortable awkwardness of the intrusive examination, the doctor listened for a heartbeat, then smiled. Mom, it sounds like you are having twins. An ultrasound verified the fact.

Say what?! Twins??? Twins don't run in either family! The excitement for me was uncontainable. Brian, more hesitant and overwhelmed with the newfound facts, kept silent. If he had reservations, he didn't say so.

He understood my elations, since we'd be the first in our families to have twins; along with some trepidation, realizing we'd have three children under two, the idea was a bit overwhelming, yet thrilling! This was the perfect plan for us.

The day we found out, was my mom's birthday. As soon as I got home, I called her! She responded with shock, and some concerns, as multiple births have a higher risk. I was not going to engage any thoughts that incurred problems; I refused to be ill at ease. This was simply a season to step into deepening my faith, trusting God with these babies. We'd only have good results after all we had gone through. I was confident that the babies would be healthy and strong.

Faith.

The pregnancy went forward, until one day, about three months after the big announcement, my water broke while at home. Brian already on his way to work, I contacted the doctor's office, who then gave firm instructions to get to the hospital. Now!

Once Brian arrived at work, the message was given to him, and he was quick to get back into the car to head home. I was packing what needed for the hospital stay. We were about five weeks from the due date, so suitcases weren't prepared yet. I gathered the necessities and prayed best I could under the circumstances.

Brian arrived home, and off we went into the next phase of our pregnancy. My mind became obscured with urgent thoughts about what was happening. It concerned us all, but I needed to stay in control and do what was needed to be done. Once at the hospital, about two hours after the water broke, I was scurried into a room, with my doctor following soon after. He did the initial check and created a plan of action to keep the babies safe and healthy. He left the room to get prepped; to my utter sadness and disappointment, a cesarean section was necessary.

Contractions were starting, with one of the sweet babies wanting to wave his way out. I felt a twitch and reacted to the odd sensation. Amused somewhat with one of them preparing me for life with twins, this one would most definitely be the clown. The twitch, kick or wave happened again. A nurse was walking in to check on me. She put her hand on my shoulder, and said with sarcasm, after I explained what I felt, "Oh, no… that's not happening, sweetie. Are you sure you're not having a seizure?" If ever I wanted to slap someone, it was that woman, at that moment.

The "look" happened, and with the sternest voice I could offer without getting mad, I stated I wanted "my" doctor, and not an intern (the intern with our first pregnancy failed epically).

I was certain these babies needed attention ASAP, since one of them was in a hurry to get out of the womb. She shook her head oh so briefly and walked out as if I didn't understand what was happening. The baby kicked again, he wanted out.

Moments later, my very favorite doctor came in. With a huge happy face, one that I trusted with my life and my babies, grinning, he asked what was happening, (after getting a briefing from the nurse about my possible seizure), I explained. He put gloves on and told me he'd be "goin' in" to check it out. Not a comfortable position at all.

Just imagine.... Doc's hand trying to move a determined leg, pushing its way out, then trying to turn such leg in the opposite direction, so the baby with his head down could come out first. This was not going to happen. (And yes, I gloated because I knew what "I" was talking about. Not the nurse who thought her degree gave her the utmost knowledge over me. Ha! Never underestimate a mother and her body!).

Oh, how I wanted to give her a piece of my mind. Thankfully, she and I were not in the same room again. All I know with that situation is God kept me from actin' a fool!

With a determined baby wanting to come out foot first, and the best effort from my doctor to deliver naturally, the c-section had to happen. We were running out of time, at the three-hour point since the water broke; two babies and one pushing his way out. I was deflated for the first time in this pregnancy. Surrealism set in. This was serious. Not how we wanted it to happen. Babies being born too early, and by C-section.

Children Are A Heritage

I felt like a failure. Moving forward with urgency, the anesthesiologist gave me a spinal. A second deflated moment, which I did not want to happen. So many horror stories had been reported with terrible outcomes of people being paralyzed from such procedure.

I questioned both doctors, and both said it was necessary under the circumstances. Again, feeling so compressed. Alone in the room, while Brian was prepping to be by my side during the surgery, I desperately wanted someone to change the scenario. Silently begging for someone to please sprinkle fairy dust to make the situation transform into something positive. I did not want fear to enter my mind, but I was concerned with the whole process.

Once the spinal was injected, everything happened so fast, seemingly chaotic. My body was numb from the shoulders down while delivering the babies. A cloth that was placed across my chest so I wouldn't see the gore and open belly area, I became taxed out, feeling claustrophobic for the first time in my life, I had to concentrate really hard on something else. Oh, how I needed some fun music played to distract me. Breathing, Lamaze, nothing seemed to ease my racing mind. Prayer should have, but my brain was whirling with too many thoughts, like guppies on steroids.

This could not be happening.

I praised the Lord and was elated to have twins. I expected a good delivery with two amazing babies. I imagined how perfect it would be to have a girl and boy. That was my hope. It was also a good possibility that it'd be our last pregnancy. That would have been the icing on the cake for us. But this was happening.

A rush of sadness and bewilderment covered me like a flood. God, what's happening, my mind asked? Help us please, were the only things I could muster up. No other words could flow during that scurrying time.

Baby A and Baby B were both boys. My mind accepted this with ease. We'd have a home filled with rambunctious lads. I was comfortable adjusting to not having a girl. They would share clothes, toys, etc. Easy. Wonderful. Perfect family at hand. They sutured me up. Brian at my head, making sure I was breathing in and out. The blur set in a few hours in the recovery room as they observed me after the delivery. The epic spinal which concerned me so much, I thought paralyzed me because I couldn't feel my legs for almost two days. It was an incredibly frightening time.

While they pushed my bed into a recovery area, I was so cold. As a warm person, I knew something was wrong, because I was shivering from within. I have always been hot blooded. The quivering made me even more uncomfortable. The staff seemed unmoved by my concerns. Nurses ignored me. I was not a happy camper. Being overly drugged, and at the point of exhaustion, I had to rely on Brian's voice, who was clueless what to do.

The spinal pushed my body over the limit. In the situation's emergence, I was overdosed from the spinal. I kept expressing how cold I was. I needed another blanket. Unaware of the fact I had a few warming blankets on me, the last time I begged for one more, yet another evil nurse

Children Are A Heritage

who stood close by, sideway glanced at me, in a half-baked way said, "No more blankets, it won't change anything." Vile, right? Oh, she was so lucky I was too worn out to ask her name and reem her out. (Oh, God protected yet again, from me actin' a fool!). I'm sure I was whining at that point. The shivering was to the point of being uncomfortable. It was abnormal. I needed someone to fight for me. Brian was perplexed. Minutes turned into hours with slow change. I seemed to warm up, but not much. The feeling in my legs were so numb for so long, I envisioned myself in a wheelchair. My imagination went wild over the next thirty-six hours. I was frightened.

During the time in recovery, my doctor, a hospital pediatrician, as well as a few other staff members, expressed that both babies were in dire condition. Delivering a month early was too premature for them to be out of the womb.

The last few weeks are critical to the nurturing of each organ in the last stage of pregnancy.

Yes, this was happening....again. Sadness took a grip.

Both at twenty-one inches long, Michael was three pounds and thirteen ounces. Mark was under two pounds. Michael was the strong, more determined of the two. There was a slim chance he would live but have deficiencies. Whisked off into the Neonatal Department, to be hooked to life-support equipment and examined, we waited. My mind and heart kept walking around the revolving door saying, "This can't be happening again."

How? There was never a mom more thrilled to have three children under two, as I was! Our family was to be

Forever HOPE

uniquely designed just as it was transpired. We had just gone through this a few years earlier. My mind felt as if tricks were being played on me. Twisted as it was, I had to process the magnitude of what was happening to us and sort out the facts. How can we deal with this, was a question I silently thought, not wanting to express the words out loud. It felt like an out-of-body experience, a movie at best, with someone else playing the lead part, because this could not be happening a second time.

I was taken to a double room, not a private room, which would have been my preference, under the circumstances. Someone was in the bed next to me. "Just great", I thought. This was not a time I wanted to share with a stranger. I dozed off. I'm guessing nurses gave her a heads up with what was happening since she kept soundless.

It was all much too surreal. Two moms give birth, and there'd normally be plenty of happy conversation to share. The typical questions should have been asked of each other, did you have a boy, girl, how much did he weigh, how'd you decide on a name type of small talk. None of that transpired. Silence. I was okay having no idle chit chat. Shut down occurred. I suppose so I wouldn't become overwhelmed. What a safety mechanism God places within us when emergency circumstances occur.

It's just the way I deal with big issues, sort out the details.... alone. My mind needed to rest and segment the W questions. Mostly the whys.

I was able to doze off for a short time. Brian left to make a few more calls, (no cell phones then, so home was the best place for privacy as he contacted family), eat dinner or nap, before coming back to the hospital. I told him I was alright to leave; it was best for me to sleep, at least I would try. There wasn't a reason for him to spend the night in an uncomfortable chair if he stayed with me. He also needed to be with our son, that would be best.

Somewhere around ten p.m. my body, still full of meds from the spinal, felt is if I were in a dream due to the grogginess; men in white coats stood at the foot of my bed and for a nanosecond, I wondered if they were coming to take me away. I sensed a few nurses in the room with said doctors; a small crowd staring at me, which felt very movie-like.

I wondered if they felt compassion, despair or did the professionalism supersede emotion? All were familiar to me; The head of neonatal spoke to tell me it looked like both babies would not live, as he continued on with what seemed like mumbo jumbo talk that made no sense, similar to Charlie Brown's mom when she speaks: Mwah mwah mwah. Nothingness. Numb was the word of the day.

I laid there as if I couldn't express any words. In my tired and half-awake mind, wondered if they cared at all about my alertness or lack of. They were doing their duty. How professional of them I thought. Could I will them away by reacting with a yes or no answer, so they understood that I was responsive. I heard what they had to say, even though I didn't want to accept the words spoken. I needed them to take their bad news anywhere else and leave me alone on the right side of the curtain, in a room I shared with a silent stranger. I was in denial.

Forever **HOPE**

While Doctor White Coat finished his words, I remember him saying, "Do you have any questions?" He tapped my foot, as if to express his condolences, I nodded. He added, for some type of assurance, my doctors would be making rounds in the morning to discuss further details. In my mind, I said, "You can leave now, I'm not some guinea pig you can watch like a science project".

I continued to feel an out of body experience, as if this wasn't really happening. Another crisis, another nightmare, like a bad movie, and I am the lead character. Everyone needed to leave the room. ALONE is all I wanted to be. Strangers had no place in my space while I live through this tragedy.

This girl does not fall apart; I process each step, like an exercise. Me, Jesus and my husband can sort out the details together. That's all that mattered. It felt as if I were walking a winding path in the dark. Only Jesus' presence would bring light into this situation.

Shortly after they all left, I fell into a light sleep. Rest. I welcomed it. It must have been around midnight when I felt someone in my room. There was something tranquil about it; it wasn't a staff member, nor a relative.

It was a quiet, peaceful entrance, discreet with a sense of sereneness that was comforting. Maureen, if I remember her name correctly, was a nurse from my OB office. She was always kind, conversational and thorough with each pregnancy checkup. Her gifting as a nurse was tender and always full of compassion. She connected with each patient. This being our third, we had a bond, I suppose, and a heart that offered empathy for what she did as a nurse; a one of a kind treasure, a true gem.

She heard what happened and specifically stopped in to check on me. If I hadn't been so exhausted emotionally and physically, I would have cried tears of appreciation for her thoughtfulness. She sat next to me, apologizing for coming in so late at night, but wanted to see how I was doing. She checked on the babies before coming into my room and found out how challenging the situation was. I believe she prayed a quiet prayer over me and expressed that I could contact her if I needed help, or just to talk. How considerate she was to take time and extend herself to me. Tears come to my eyes as I remember the sweetest of gestures. What an amazing outpouring of love she offered to me. This was not just a professional, but someone with a heart bigger than her job. She made sure staff tended to me. I knew I had someone with medical know-how on my side if help was needed. I knew I would get through the night because she took the time to offer support.

Although I did not want to sun to shine, morning did rise from the dark night. The soreness was setting in, I could finally feel more of my legs, but still concerned I'd be in a wheelchair. The staff continued to be unbothered by my concern of lack of movement in my legs, twenty-four hours later. Not good. But I am grateful God heard my heart cry and knew my thoughts as I silently prayed over that twenty-four-hour time frame to feel movement again.

Over the next few days, we walked through the danger zone with both babies, waiting for more tests to be done.

The doctors suggested to us that our immediate family come up to meet the babies before they "expire", as if they were quarts of milk.

Keeping it intimate and less of a spectacle, only our parents visited. It would help them through the grief process.

Strange. Odd. Looming. What should have been a joyous time of celebrating the sweet birth of our babies, instead, sadness lurked its ugly shadow over us. The heavy storm cloud hovered only to offer us despair and anguish.

Brian and I sat by "Baby A", who was hooked up and under an oxygen tent. Monitors beeping to many different rhythms, he had a small ray of hope. He was our foot first child, a very stubborn fighter, the larger of the two, who we found out might live after all. Doctors and nurses explained he'd have a long road, but there began a slight possibility of survival. The outlook was still grim at best, we held on with confidence and many vigilant prayers.

Hope was ours after all.

Baby "B" had no brain waves, nor were his organs developed. Sitting on the chair next to him, in discomfort with stitches running up and down my stomach from the C-Section, I gazed at his sweet little face, tiny feet and hands, and huge eyes. "How could this be happening?" was the only thought that ran endlessly through my mind.

We weren't the only family struggling with these questions, as my eyes couldn't bypass the many other babies in incubators all around me. The beeping noises, wires and monitors where overbearing to this momma's soul. I wanted to fix them all and make each of them strong and healthy

Children Are A Heritage

so there would be no need for a neonatal department, ever. Too many parents going through their own struggles with each baby having a set of medical diagnoses to deal with. We weren't walking this path alone, but my mind wanted to refute it all. How unfair to see each baby struggling to stay alive.

Baby "B", was hooked up to life support... *life support....a baby*. Such necessity is for old people and those who are really sick. He would "live", lifelessly, until we were prepared to turn off the machine that kept him "alive".

Pangs hit hard, straight to the heart of this momma.

No parent should ever have to make such decisions when to turn off the switch to keep their child alive on this earth. Especially not for a newborn; this was so incredibly unfair. Life is wretched. It felt like I was playing God. Brian couldn't do it.

Words again were few. There were no weighty discussions. No screaming, although I wanted to run up and down the hospital corridors yelling at the top of my lungs as loud as I could, simply for the sake of burning off energy that I did not want to hold in.

Brian, I don't think, could verbalize the pain. (Is this a man thing? I suppose it was). He was supportive, but more than his heart could endure, as my heart pined with great intensity. Yearning for a better outcome, we had to face the inescapable fact, picking the "best time" to turn off this innocent baby's lifeline.

We somehow, as one, the way only a husband and wife would understand, had to take small steps, dealing with

Forever HOPE

the unavoidable, with few words spoken. Yet, I knew, even with the momentary angst of the situation, God comforted me and gave me assurance to not let my heart be distressed but trust Him.

I accepted contentment because He surrounded me with compassion and love. Though the depth of my being wanted to grow wings and fly away, dismissing all the bad happening within my emotions, I was desperately trying not to lose control. God. He was in control. I would again, find the peace that passes all understanding.

We made it through this repeated situation, just a short two years earlier. We were prepared to make the appropriate connections to arrange a funeral.

We made it through the first full day of our twins' life. Many doctors and nurses offered information and solace. We telephoned a local funeral home, who took care of all required arrangements for our baby. Such a relief. Numbness set in over those days, as we walked out our adult life, preparing another baby's funeral.

This was a part of who I was. My story. Why was I chosen to be the strong one, I often asked God? From my heart to God's ears, many questions were offered up. Comfort was the assurance given during those difficult days. Leaning into God brought peaceful healing, which didn't happen overnight. But I learned to run, not walk into my Father's Arms for consolation. He is the Author of my life's story. I have to believe that or not. If I do, I can accept and learn, even in difficulties, worries and problems thrown

Children Are A Heritage

my way. Discouragement and sadness would have to flee because the peace God gave me flooded my soul.

Our first baby was easier because I had a normal delivery, even in its prolonged state. This cesarean section was for the birds. I wouldn't wish the experience on anyone. It took what seemed like forever to recover.... and a huge lifetime scar would be a continuous reminder of the difficulty endured, as a token that replaced the life I should have been blessed with. I've often said, I'd rather give birth to a porcupine then go through another cesarean. No, thank you!

On day three of the twin's lives, it was time to turn the life-giving switch to the off position. Our parents had time to meet this precious baby. Funeral arrangements were made, then the moment arrived to walk to the bedside of precious "Baby B", whom we named Mark. There was a surreal flood of emotion roaring inside of me, yet there was a surrender, because of the peace Jesus put inside my heart. The battle that raged, belonged to Jesus. He was my refuge during the bereavement time.

How does a parent choose when their baby will die?

The doctors gave us the option to turn off the life support switch. We could have left the room for the doctors to complete the daunting task; but we wanted to be with Mark when the knob was turned to the off position, and he ascended to heaven. He would be with his brother Bryan.

Was that a consolation? In some strange and uncomfortable way, it offered a solace.

The doctors and nurses waited politely around the corner, for privacy, as we said our goodbyes, with a silent whisper.

Reeling in unbelief, wishing it all away, we released Mark into the arms of Jesus. Silently. Quietly. Emotions ran deep from Brian and me; I felt as if a lion were ripping the heart out of my chest.

The immense sadness and closure weighted heavy, yet there was a blanketing peace within. Amid the overwhelming process, Jesus brought comfort to us, on this dark and difficult day.

Two pieces of my heart were in heaven that day. Our babies together, as I imagined Jesus holding one in each arm. The assurance was mine, they were in the best place of all, as my heart felt the weight like a bowling ball, missing the opportunity to be a mom to them, and watch them grow into adulthood, would never happen.

There is always hope amid any storm. I hold to that evidence still today. Strings of hope. Jesus. Redeemer and my Comforter. He welcomed my baby into heaven and introduced him to his brother Bryan. I'm sure they started a soccer team, their daddy's favorite sport.

Brian watched my confidence in God through these weighty experiences, which never wavered. He never said as much, but he had to have wondered when the bomb would drop, and I'd lose a gasket or two. I never did. Jesus remains my Rock and stability.

What was the comfort I held onto? It was the sweet images of heaven that made me smile. Conceptualizing our babies as a welcoming committee one day in the distant future, when we would meet again. I had babies here on earth that needed me. I never felt a total loss, in the sense of wanting to die in the midst of all we went through during those years. People often struggle with anguish after the death of someone dear. There is always a void. That link is gone from this earth. Yet life still continues while on this earth.

My mind knowing eternity is forever, offers great comfort that I will spend forever with my babies. This earth, at best gives us, if all goes accordingly, seventy-five to a hundred years. I get the better deal later. So, to put the situation into perspective, I relish the time I get to spend with the children gifted to me on this earth. Comfort. Joy. Peace. All precious gifts no one can take away, not even the enemy of my soul.

Tears came and went with each baby. The heartache lessened in time. Brian continued to quietly observe with periodic questions about faith, and why I trusted in the unseen. There were times in conversation with people in general, brave enough to ask how I endured what we went through, insisting they would have fallen apart. I'd explain, suffering happens to everyone, but it brings endurance and strength, which deepens the character in a person, and keeps hope alive.

God never brings sadness nor depression onto people. But he pours his heart into our lives through the Holy Spirit if we receive that. So, I rejoice, and trust God like never before. These are the times faith is indeed tested. Growing stronger in Him, digging into the Bible, seeking answers to problems, and yes, some questions left unanswered, I was learning more each day of His faithfulness.

Forever HOPE

Brian struggled with numerous matters, ill at ease with his faith; yet, somehow in my heart, I knew he was leaning into the truth that God had us in the palm of His hands. God gave me this gift of peace that the world cannot offer. I will not be afraid nor troubled when things happen to me, or around me.

When I was released to go home, desperate to be with Christopher, and so grateful for his eighteen-month-old sweetness, I needed his hugs as much as he needed mine. Pieces from the void of not having our baby needed to be put together like a puzzle. Recuperation from surgery and healing from an infection that set within the sutures was my focus. Wondering if the pain would ever quit, strength was needed, as I eagerly anticipated a normal schedule again. I was quick to understand during this time, it was too late to expect ordinary in this extraordinary life of mine.

The day of the funeral arrived. It was a simple and quiet ceremony, with immediate family only. I questioned again why this had to be an out-of-body experience, as I sat looking at this small casket. It was numbing. Simple yet blurred. The fuzziness of it all, I silently wished it all away. I didn't want to acknowledge I was there, nor did I want to deal with it. Momentary denial. I don't remember the words said during the short service. Nor do I remember clearly what we did after. The mind is so complex. I suppose it was too much to bear, in the feeble mind.

The support of my church family offered prayers that released angels to encompass us while we walk through the grief process. People we knew came to clean and brought dinners. Not to be redundant, but peace became a friend within my soul and brought a sense of security. Anger never released its ugly head. At least, not to my remembrance. Justifiably so, it would be a normal response. We also had Michael to concentrate on. Having him gain weight and become stronger so he could come home as quickly as possible became a short-term goal. We needed to move forward as a family. Let the surreal dissipate; we yearned for normalcy

Brian continued asking me how and why I believed the Bible to be the real truth. I didn't realize he was watching my life, with a fine-toothed comb; and how I reacted to the bumps, bruises and unwelcomed life disasters we had experienced. He was keenly aware of my faith, which was solid and unwavering, compared to what he learned in his youth. I saw no changes in him when it came to faith. He was curious and asked me questions, often spoken in the middle of the night. I continued to pray with a close set of Prayer Warrior Moms, who agreed he'd come to understand God and His Word. I also prayed for God to work in Brian and allow the Holy Spirit to answer those deep questions he struggled with. I prayed the veil which keet him from God's freedom would fall away, and he'd receive God's truth. This was my deepest desire.

Day after day, for four months, we drove to the hospital to be with Michael. We saw how stubborn this baby would be (and appreciated his strength and resolve to fight). This little guy just was not eating enough to gain weight. He needed to be at five pounds before being released to come home, yet, just could not put the weight on. To his defense, they pricked and prodded him more than any baby should ever have been. Every hour or two, he had blood drawn, medicine and vitamins along with feedings from which he became too tired to eat since he couldn't get a sleep pattern set, due to his environment. It was a tough schedule for sure, but he was tougher, and we were glad he had that stubborn streak to keep him growing stronger every day.

The nurses loved him and told me so, and often! They all wanted their rocking time with Michael. He was the little ladies' man, at the ripe age of a week old. I saw that as God's favor over his life. Not that the other babies were any less loved, I'm sure they were. Maybe the nurses sang these accolades to all moms, to make us each feel at ease, offering a safe assurance because we had to leave our babies in such incubated states for so long. It was not an easy choice to walk out of the room, allowing someone else to be a surrogate mom, leaving our baby(s) into their care, all wired up and laying under an oxygen tent. This was not an experience for the weak at heart.

God was creating a brand new strength within me; I was becoming more courageous, as I walked out this Christian life on purpose. Through these monumental, life-giving, life-taking away moments, depression played no part in my life. There were tears. Sadness like a heavy cloud came in waves sometimes. But the reality would hit me, as I read my bible, or listened to a message on pain or discouragement, and I knew I had to open my heart, look up, praise God, and joy would then enter into my mind, heart and soul. If I didn't, the situation would have been unbearable. Hope was mine.

Mike came home the week before Thanksgiving. He was just shy of four months old. So many prayer vigils took place. The urgency was genuine; he needed to be healthy enough to come home. So, when he came home, we were beyond grateful to have our family of four under one roof. Brian and I were feeling stronger. Even though sadness lingered as we missed our twin that should have been home with us. We were on the mend and looking forward to a new season in life.

Michael would get sick often, as his lungs were underdeveloped, which was the main reason he stayed in the hospital so long. He was not only bigger than his twin, but his organs were all developed. As his lungs strengthened over time, I trusted God to heal him fully. With much prayer and the refusal to have an unhealthy child, we saw God answer our prayers, as Michael was healing, not all at once, but over the course of a few years. The days I became too tired, overwhelmed and disheartened when he did get sick, hope would slip from me, like holding onto a freshly cooked noodle. It was then, my Spiritual Mom's would step up as prayer warriors and pray for our family. I am forever grateful for these women, who walked out Godly lives, not perfectly, but diligently. They were the real deal. Prayers were answered, every time we called on Jesus, and trusted him to help us.

Brian and I had many conversations during Michael's pregnancy and beyond, whether to try for a girl. Brian never said as much, in his quiet nature, he had concerns. Three pregnancies, two live births, two deaths. He, along with our family, wondered if we should attempt having one more child. Our solution was, to wait five years, at that point decide if we wanted to try again for a sweet girl full of pudding and pie. I would have been close to thirty at that point, still young enough to have one more pregnancy. Our theory was, maybe, waiting, the God of all fertility would move things around, and spit out the girl code.... until Brian said: "It'd be nice to have a princess; we'd name her Angel". My immediate response: Noooooooooo!

No way would that take place! Never. No princess, no angel at my house! God must have laughed, as he whispered, "Ok, you got it. All boys it is." So, God created the Balsa Clan to be one female, the most important female, Momma girl. Nine months after we welcomed Michael into the world, a surprise baby was brewing.

It didn't take place in our ideal five-year plan, but, for a few moments during those early weeks of pregnancy, I speculated this would, for certain, be our last child, even though we wanted to wait. Thoughts rushed through my mind with the "what if" questions. You may wonder right about now, could this baby carry? Most of our family seemed uncomfortable with this pregnancy. Naturally, I understand. But I had no concerns about the actual delivery of another child. I knew this pregnancy would be fine. It was never a health issue we encountered in previous pregnancies. It was simply odd circumstances that varied from the norm. Odd situations occur in life, and we had two events that were just that. Oh, the many family members with no faith. Only worry. I prayed for them. They needed God's peace. My biggest take away from the season of having babies was – it was less of me, more of God. I never wavered in my confidence to deliver a healthy baby. We had hoped for a girl, knowing this would be our last child.

There was a lesson learned during those years while we were creating our tribe. I understood the concern about us being pregnant but worry meant we diminish what God had planned for our family. There are no accidents. God never misses a beat. What comes to harm us, gives us the chance to rebound and become stronger – in Christ. Staying focused on Him and trusting God, offered opportunities to speak of His faithfulness to others. Anxiety weighs us down. Hope offers freedom and peace. I did have moments of sadness, sometimes despair, but I rebounded. Sometimes bouncing back quickly, other times it took days, maybe weeks, but I refused to wallow in fear and sadness. God is always in control. Sometimes we hold onto our concerns too tightly. When we release them, God can then do what only He can do. So, in this last pregnancy we had, I knew this baby was meant to be ours. God had plans for our family, he was the icing on the cake, the caboose to our train. He completed us and made us whole.

It was all very wonderful! Three children, each less than two years apart, our household would be how it should be with five people. Yes, this was the end of our era, and it was worth every moment we went through, no matter the outcome, X or Y. He or She would complete our little family. #happy #complete #rejoice.

This growing bean inside of me was full of somersaulting, fist punching, soccer kicking, and swimming laps in my womb the entire nine months. I was certain this baby must be a girl. My other pregnancies were quiet, nice, easy and relaxed the whole term, only doing an occasional stretch and yawn. This bouncing baby was non stoppable, so different from the other pregnancies. The countdown to delivery came near, Brian would be surprised at delivery to find out if he had his "princess" …. or not; he wanted to find out at the birth, not one second earlier. I needed to find out before I was given the mask, what this wild child's gender was. "Yes, give me the gas, I said to the doctor," as we discussed that I'd be asleep during delivery. I refused to have another spinal after the previous ordeal. I continued to explain to the doctor, I'd be running after this running child forever, so give me a few minutes of rest, and I needed to be first to know if it was indeed a girl. I drove myself to the doctor's office the day before delivery, to have baby checked out and go over any necessary details for the birth. I do not know how I drove my big belly forty-five minutes to the office, and back home again! Upon arrival, I plopped my round moving belly on the little table in the OB room, as the final checkup progressed before bubbly baby was to be born.

"Well, Mom," said the doctor, "all looks good." He continued to inform me the baby was positioned just right, looking quite healthy and ready to be born. He then asked if I wanted to know the gender. Yes, as I took a deep breath, with anticipation and certainty that a little girl announcement was to be made, only to hear, "It's a boy!"

Ya sure, Doc? For real?? Yes indeed, no question, baby blue it is!

Needless to say, my bubble was burst. I'm sure my face gave the look of disappointment. If the doctor made any more comments after the declaration, I was unaware and disappointed. This was the final hurrah, and I would never be blessed with a girl. Having another baby later, was not an option. This was it. (Please don't shame me for being sad in the moment, because I knew the final outcome was and is really good... really, really good!)

In the forty-five-minute drive home, tears flowed gently down my cheeks, my heart crushed, knowing I'd never experience what it would be like to have a girl to buy dolls for, nor put ribbons in the hair of this imagined little girl. Nor would we play makeup and nails together. We'd never live through the heartache experience of broken relationships, when her Mr. Prince goes in a different direction, leaving her behind in tears until she finds her Mr. Right.

Arriving home, wiping my tears, and putting on my best game face, I took a deep breath before getting out of the car, walked into the house, with no words to say. I tried to act nonchalant. Brian was walking out from the kitchen, and he glanced at me. He may have said something, I don't remember; I think it was just the look a husband gives his wife when he reads her face; my mind was clouded, I went to the bathroom to wash my face with a cool cloth, came out and went on with the rest of the day.

As we drove to the hospital for the scheduled appointment for the C-Section, Brian spoke first as we were in route.

He asked, "It's not a girl, is it?"

I looked at him, a bit surprised, and sheepishly asked, "How did you know?"

His response was simple and knowing. "You weren't smiling and joyful when you came home from the doctor's office. If it was a girl, you'd have been happy."

I put my head down. Selfish, I thought, did it really matter? I may have said that out loud before getting to the hospital. But my heart wanted a girl to create those momma daughter memories and moments I never had with my mom. I would be determined to do better with my daughter. But it was a closed chapter. God had other plans.

Tears fill my eyes even now as I write this chapter. Knowing I missed out on all that would have gone on with raising a daughter, princess or not. The fun, laughter, tears, and yes, even the hormones (to which I'd have to add, boys, have crazy hormones, too!).

With great joy, and a heart overflowed, a few hours later, bouncing baby Jonathan, entered our space, with a loud screaming cry that announced into the airwaves of the delivery room, that he was here to shake our world just like he did in the womb for nine long months. I smiled at the sound, while I realized it all went well.

This child, our caboose, is the boy that never stopped. Our go-getter, a leader and commander in charge everywhere he went. We wouldn't have exchanged his life for a host of daughters.

I love this boy, now a man, with all my being. My cup was full of life with our other two sons, but Jonathan was the surplus for our family; always a barrel bursting with passionate energy. Life is good, and our family was complete. We'd have it no other way.

God knows the gifts we need to have in our life, including children, which are a blessing from the Lord. #grateful. #lovebeingamomofboys

Forever HOPE
Water from the Well

- How can we trust God, especially in the midst of loss?
- Have you wondered what it must have been like for God to send his only Son to this earth? Knowing the brutality, rejection, pain, hurt and extreme suffering he'd go through. God did that for you and me! The One True God, Son of Man, Son of God, died the most brutal deaths, at the hands of people. Rejection and anguish came on him, to offer freedom and the opportunity to say yes to Heaven and all it has for us. This is the promise we have. Even when we walk through the valley of death, no fear can come on us (unless we allow it, by choice). He comforts us, because he experienced pain, like us. Jesus blesses those who by choice, choose Him as Savior. Our cup runs over. Our paths are made straight. His beauty and love chase us every day so we can look forward to eternity. Those that go to heaven before us will be there to greet us. That brings great joy!

- The Holy Spirit is gentle. He covers us like a blanket with his comfort, in only the way He could. Nothing in this world can offer the security of God, no matter what circumstances rise up in our life.
- The Bible is our guide to help us live more like him, especially when we go through tough times. The Why's of life can be answered when we quiet ourselves to hear God's voice; this often times come in the way of comfort in our heart. Peace sets in. Even when we don't know the exact purposes of our loss, He does. Learn from Teacher. His plan for you is to give hope.
- How can you implement the acceptance of his perfect love in your heart today? Tomorrow?
- Where does your hope come from?
- Peace that passes all understanding can be yours when you live a life with Christ.

MARRIAGE, FAMILY AND LIFE

Love should be patient and kind

From the beginning of our marriage, Brian would oftentimes wake me in the middle of the night to ask me Bible questions. Let me re-emphasize, he was an early morning person, and I am a late-night owl. When he'd decided he couldn't sleep, he would wake me somewhere around two in the morning, as I had gotten to sleep shortly before these awakenings! Silently, in my mind, I would say "why in the middle of the night do we need to converse?" But, I realized, in my sleepiness, God was working in my husband in a deep and profound way.

If I am honest, my responses spoken, were in a grungy nighttime gremlin voice (imagine that!), how loving and attractive, right? And more important, this momma needed her beauty sleep!! I'd offer a semi begrudged answer, half awake, then try to fall back into lalaland.

In time, I realized, it was less threatening for him, to ask questions in the midnight's dark hour. You know those nights when the mind races like a machine in high gear, yet we desperately need to sleep, and can't turn off the wiring within our head. I'm certain, this was that!

In simple terms, I gave him an answer that came down to faith. Trust. Prayer. God's Word was true, it had to be true. No other option was available. Be resolute in what you believe. I knew my confidence was in God and not circumstances. Further explaining to Brian, we either take faith as an action word or we don't. Then the ultimate question he'd wondered, was why bad things happen in the world. Simply answered, God allows people the freedom to choose.

I tried to convey with each conversation how God offers an unmovable assurance. Which is anchored in Christ. The Bible is and was the truth, and that is the only way I got through the hard times. He believed that and rested in it. The Holy Spirit was prompting his uncertain faith, all the while, I didn't see the evidence of what was transpiring.

The despondent differences in our denominations, were contrasting neon lights, to say the least. The sense of obligation he felt so deep to the church he grew up in, which rejected us when we got married, left a hole in his heart.

I also expressed that when seeking God's answer, find wisdom in sound guidance, the Bible, prayer and a quiet ear to hear His voice.

Years went by, there were no spiritual changes in him. I was digging into the Word of God with all that I had, always wishing and praying I had more time to learn and share the

Word with him. I loved God's word, more than life itself. As I studied the Bible, my faith and hope grew deeper and stronger as time went on. This was indeed the life I loved. Not the world and nonsense in it. So many problems surrounded us in our life, in relationships and everyday living. I knew we needed God more each day. God is the problem solver in the midst of whatever came our way. We always got through, no matter the situation.

Brian endured the spiritual struggle from within his soul. It was heart-wrenching to watch, day after day. I held on to hope that he would overcome the tension from the law-abiding rules they taught him, vs. the true freedom Jesus offers us. To be honest, some days were more difficult to trust God with my husband's life. I wanted to fix it for him. He needed the freedom that only Jesus offers.

Fast forward to New Year's Eve of the year we celebrated our fifteenth anniversary, and eighteen years of being together. We had our share of normal life problems. We shared much laughter, joy, jokes, and silliness; we were best friends, although oddly different, but we thrived in our core values, which is what merged us together years earlier. Family was a priority. We laughed, even with different styles of humor, his being very dry, and I was always cracking up at the silliest of things with loud bouts of laughter. Life was at least interesting. Together, we were not the average couple, and that was ok.

I was slowly losing hope, concerned he would not receive the freedom Jesus offers when prayed for it to happen. My grip was not as secure as it was years earlier, in my determination he would realize the differences in our walk with God, accept liberty and understand God's sovereignty I personally grew into. The Brian was in a spiritual headlock, and my flesh was becoming impatient. In some sense, the occasional creepy feeling to give up slithered into my mind. The flesh can be relentless. When I prayed, sometimes it was just a whimper, from the early stronger and determined younger days when I prayed for this man of mine. I was to the point of giving up with no prospect we might be yoked as one wholly and purified in biblical standards.

Never be disenchanted when a person proclaims to be a Christian, that he or she morph into this perfected human robot. That's the farthest thing from the truth. We lose hope sometimes, we feel sad, we say or do things that we should not. The Bible tells us that no one is perfect but God. What we do have is the firm foundation that Salvation is ours when we ask. Anytime the ray of hope seems to have dissipated never give up, not on your husband nor loved ones! Keep praying with a gentle teaching spirit. They will inherit the blessing and hope.

Growth is a process. We do not arrive until we get to Heaven. There were many days, that I felt Brian was holding on to 'my faith', because I did not waiver from what I believed. He was indeed watching. When I did not see the change, I realized that I had to let go of wanting to fix him. It's a tough thing to do, I admit it. As an oldest/only child, I am a fixer by nature. I want to help. When I see a problem, I want to bring it to the surface to make the changes. I hate to see failure. But it is sometimes inevitable. I had to let my husband find his own salvation in Jesus.

This particular year, our pastor planned a family communion for New Year's Eve. Each family set an appointed time to have communion, prayer, and blessing, with him. It was a sweet one-on-one time to reflect over the year past, with prayerful hearts as we entered the new year. I signed our family up, if I remember, for the eleven-p.m. slot. The boys were eight, ten and twelve and thought it was *so cool* we'd be going to church "in the middle of the night"! Oh, the joys and simple things that made them happy! I was unsure if Brian would join us. But my pastor and I agreed as we prayed, he would feel welcomed to join in this family event.

The conundrum was whether Brian would feel free to join us, due to the kibosh put on him to not take communion because I wasn't part of his denomination. They didn't accept our marriage, according to the guidelines of his church. Brian struggled with that for fifteen years.

It meant so much to him, as he took his relationship with God seriously, and respectfully. It was discouraging for him to not be able to receive communion since it is a valuable part of the Christian walk. I watched his continence diminish over those years when would talk about the Bible and God. He struggled watching my peace with God, as he attempted to find his own, so unsuccessfully, due to the words spoken over our lives sixteen years earlier.

I lived with the frustration of that spiritual fight all those years, not willing to hold on to it any longer. I continued to grow in God, learning the Bible's instructions were correct and not man-made laws. My spiritual life was tangible and secure, that would never change.

When the boys and I came home from church that afternoon, we told him about the event, along with the timeslot chosen. I was casual, not wanting him to feel pressured, but desperately longing for him to join the boys and me. The ache in my heart was deep, as I hoped for my husband to be the head of our family spiritually. I longed for the time we would read the Bible, pray and attend Sunday services together. It was a vivid vision I held onto and replayed often in my mind. I was still holding on to that image of the white picket fence, filled with all the beauty God offered us.

Ok, don't laugh at my dream. Come on now, I wanted the white picket fence–I still hope to have that one day!!! I'm certain God laughs at all of us with a great sense of humor. Yes, I believe God has some good belly laughs with us and at our dreams.

New Year's Eve approached, the boys were bouncing off the wall, so excited that we'd be going out to church, in the *nighttime hours*. Elated and willing, they had their clothes and shoes prepared for this monumental event.

Brian had fallen asleep earlier, as was normal for him since his mornings began around 4:30 a.m. I expected him to sleep on through the night, as he always had done. I reminded him, at dinner, as did the boys, with all the pent-up energy they had, the timeframe we needed to leave for church. I'm sure the boys tried to wake him at some point to remind him to get dressed. Whether he got up or not, we were preparing to keep our appointed time at church.

But as we were nearing the time to leave for church, Brian was dressed, tie and all. With a sheepish look, he quietly asked if he could still come with. *He was asking me?!?! Realllly?!??!* Trying to act all nonchalant, I nodded, as the boys were full of energy, rambunctious and ready to go. Did this man of mine not realize that my insides were jumping up and down, with more excitement than my kids were at that very moment!??? Not sure if I acted that "chilled", or if he indeed saw the joy overflowing within me, which must have been spouting out my ears, eyes, nose and belly button.

Shortly after that heart filled moment, full of surprise, I silently prayed for the new year to be our best year as a family. I put on my coat, hat, and gloves to enter into the cold winter night, for our family communion. All the while, that charming picket fence in my mind was being ordered, and ready to be put up. I knew God was doing a new thing in our family. I was grateful beyond words.

We drove the ten-minute drive to church, pulled up to a cozy, low lit building with a communion table ready to serve, with our pastor waiting. I could see his blue eyes humbly sparkle, with a caring grin and welcoming hello, before we entered the foyer. I recognized that he, too, was thankful for answered prayers as Brian walked into the church with us. Our hearts connected through the souls of our eyes. God is good. He never gives up on anyone. Especially a praying wife, with an agreeing pastor!

Forever HOPE

I savored those few moments, wishing it to last much longer. The lights low for a gentle ambiance, set the mood as we held the "Bread and Cup". With humbled hearts, we thanked God for the previous year and asked for his mighty provision for the new year. Life felt so complete at that moment, as we held hands as a family. So much so, I wanted to freeze frame time. The yearning to request life to stay this peaceful and in sync flowed through my heart. The tenderness of this very monumental and special evening brought me great joy.

The boy's energy dwindled as we drove home. Brian thanked me for including him. (In my mind, I said to myself: *Like I wouldn't have?!? Come on now!*) New Year's Day came and went. Time seemed to speed along as fast as lightning; school resumed after the holiday break and our schedules were back on track, busy as ever. It was somewhere in those following weeks when Brian said, not so much as a reminder, but as a fact that he had not taken communion for over sixteen years; (believe me, I didn't need to be reminded of the religious anguish he endured through the previous years). He sensed a change in his heart as he received communion; thanking me, because it meant the world to him to have this peace he encountered on New Year's Eve. It touched me more than I can express on this page. His tender words moved me. What a fragrant moment in his life, and I was honored that I was there to share this precious moment. His countenance had changed. God was in the midst. Prayers were being answered.

In my mind, I reflected on life and its experiences. Situations taint or bless our heart. I received communion, with no bars held. I suppose I took it for granted, this precious gift of Jesus Christ's body, for my sins. An act, that we as Christians should always take seriously, and often. Taking time to humble ourselves at His Throne, realizing that Jesus accepted the responsibility to walk down the road called Golgotha, as a sacrifice for all of us is a major part of our Christian walk. The horrendous pain and suffering that Jesus bore, so we can be saved, by His blood, to be healed so we might worship him. Communion is a time to thank him for giving us himself, as a sacrifice for the sins created on the earth.

As we go to communion, it's a surrendering and letting go of our strong will, so we can be cleansed and forgiven of our shortcomings.

Sin occurs every day. It can be a simple lie, murder, or anything in-between. Sin is sin is sin. None of us can throw a stone at someone else without realizing we have to point the finger at our self too. No one is exempt. No one. But we, through Grace, and His wisdom that completes us, can believe every word the Bible says. [So, how do we fix it? Extend grace to our self and to others, by helping address the problems we know are sinful; correct the situation in love, not in anger. Sometimes, we need to challenge someone, or even our self, when we are willingly doing wrong. Grace comes when we turn away from sin, ask God to forgive us, and He will!]

We grow and have our being to become more like him every day. This is what Brian missed out on, for those fifteen years; the battle was real and apparent. It cut into the core of his soul. It was so uncalled for and pointless; a trigger of the enemy of his soul to gain access into his mind and heart to create a torment of sorts.

The giants in his life needed to come down so he could live without condemnation. He needed confidence that came from the One who created him. The Light of Jesus began to change Brian's life that New Year's Eve night. There was a subtle glow from the inside out. The sweetness of God is using Brian's life, through this story.

In obedience, as I share these details with you, I hope you get a glimpse of how God wastes nothing in situations we live through. He used Brian to refine my life. He will use things in your life, too. The good, the bad, and the ugly. It all can serve a purpose, if we breathe and accept that God offers us freedom from within.

The strength I had was in Christ, not anyone else's salvation. I shared this amazing promise from God with a husband who watched me through our deepest darkest days. This could have easily kept us in despair. He was searching for peace.

God stayed faithful to us. He used our weakest experiences to gain strength and developed our unique storyline called life; we grew in Him because we allowed him to. If we fight it, deny it, push it down, refuse to live through the pain, it stays hidden like a needle in a haystack.

When we live in God, and know Jesus, we can take communion; it is a free gift, given by the blood of Jesus. He set the captive free. Brian needed inner freedom; he didn't know how to get what the Lord had for him. It was a battle of the mind and heart. He had finally stepped into that freedom. Answers to prayer were happening before my eyes.

Little did I know what God was doing in him during this season. He had struggles he still battled in personal ways; but the enemy hated that Brian was seeking the truth. The One Truth. The enemy doesn't go down without a fight. (Beware, we as Christ followers do have an opposer).

The days went by. Weeks turned into months. Spring was in the air, with an opportunity for the ladies at church to put together a skit welcoming people to the Banquet Table. Our Pastor and his wife shared this story at our church which offered an opportunity for us to invite guests to the church. I was approached to be part of the cast; I hadn't been in front of a crowd to speak since English class in high school, which left me a bit nervous and apprehensive. I hesitated to accept this small task since I'm not one to memorize lines. But I was definitely drawn to taking part in this presentation. (I am certain God was doing the nudging). The cast was chosen, practice dates created for our calendar, as we prepared to share "the story".

The Saturday before the skit, we practiced our lines and set the table up with beautiful linens, china and teacups. I was a bit nervous, as I wanted to make sure my lines were memorized well. Everything was arranged. We were as ready as we could be and excited to see what God was going to accomplish through us.

You can find the storyline in Luke 14:15-24, which explains the intimacy of Christ leading the conversation as he sat at the table with his friends. He offered yet another analogy, as he did so well, desiring us to be blessed when we eat bread in the Kingdom of God. The invitation was offered to all. And, in true fashion, the story tells us how, as people often do, even in today's age, the excuses made as to why they could not be at the feast. One needed to tend to his land; another had his oxen to take care of; one more had to be with his wife. It seemed to be of no importance for these folks to take time to eat with Jesus where there would be a bounty of food and enjoy His companionship.

The person hosting the dinner became angry, telling his slave to go out into the streets of the city and bring in the poor, crippled, blind and lame. Yet there was still plenty of food left for more to come and eat. The Master commanded to the slave to go back out again, along the highway and compel these people to join in for the banquet. (There must have been a lot of food!)

The custom was for the banquet dinner to be a time of celebration, with good food that was plentiful, but included in the feast was music, fellowship and laughter. The story reminds me of a wedding reception we might do in todays' culture, even a Christmas gathering offers an abundance of food and gifts.

Memories created with family and friends are priceless, so we want everyone to be a part of the occasion. Within that time and culture, to be a regular person, invited to come to a wealthy person's home, just didn't happen. Those who were on the A list, who refused the request of attending the dinner, must have been a bit of a mockery to the host.

Jesus wanted the group to understand, it's not just food we eat and the gathering together, but the Kingdom of God is ours when we eat the Bread of His Life.

That was our heart, that Sunday morning. Extending to those who would be at church with us, to sense the welcome mat, accept this Banquet of Jesus' sweet and tender love, that overflows to anyone. All we need to do is say yes to Him.

The boys and I left home early to prepare for the skit. Brian arrived when the service started. Excitement filled the room, in hopes that our few guests would hear the sweet message of Jesus and accept him as Savior that morning. We prayed, as it should be, when any message of the Gospel was shared. God doesn't need permission to touch lives, but our willing heart to put Him first in our activities. What we desired was to allow the Holy Spirit to be present.

The performance went well; the picturesque long table set up in pristine fashion, set the mood brilliantly. The skit went off with only a few line glitches, but nothing catastrophic. Pastor completed the message, and if I recall, we finished service a little early that day; I was a happy girl, and proud of myself for accepting this feat. I conquered a fear, which made it easier to stand up in front of groups of people to speak when future opportunities were offered. God was doing a new thing in me.

Forever **HOPE**

After service, the ladies and I stayed behind to pack the props used. Brian and I met up in the middle of the sanctuary with onlookers watching, in hopes to see his reaction....... *no pressure at all*! I asked him if we did well; he replied with a yes, expressing that everyone did a good job. He took the boys with him, as I'd be home soon after the clean-up. We gave a little kiss goodbye, and I had a good sense that he enjoyed the storyline.

As the church cleared out, a group of ladies and I bundled the glassware, and folded linens, which made me feel like we were in an 1890s scene of Little House on the Prairie. These ladies chuckled like schoolgirls that my husband kissed me goodbye.... in the sanctuary! I sheepishly wondered what was so special about that–asking at least one friend what the big deal was. It wasn't like we were making out in the church parking lot! It was a small peck, as he left for home.

Evidently, my church girlfriends didn't have husbands who would kiss them in church. No public display of affection, especially in the sanctuary, oh my! Again, this became one of those little memories I look back on and remember fondly. (Reminder ladies, no PDA in church). I smile as I reflect on this memory.

We giddily complimented each other on a job well done. Some ladies asked if Brian understood the message offered to the audience. I shared that in that quick moment before he left, he stated that the message was clear, and it was a job well done.

Once home, Brian, sensed my contained energy and pleasure bursting at the seams. He affirmed how well I and the other ladies had completed such an unnerving task, with this being my first-time acting experience. He knew my apprehension; I am sure he prayed that I would do well that morning.

We talked over lunch, as our kids ate and then ran off to play and through the conversation, Brian said overall, it was put together nicely. The stage was set; we spoke loudly enough for the audience to hear, and although few of us had some delayed moments, nothing catastrophic transpired. I pushed him more, to get his take on the storyline, wanting to verify he understood the message.

He got it. Jesus wants us to sit with him, to receive the full benefits of himself in us. But we have to accept him, say yes to the invitation. He is calling each person to himself. The food is an analogy to our spiritual needs. We must say yes to Jesus, taking his hand, and desire to rest in Him, enjoying life and all it offers.

My heart was bursting. God was answering prayer, as I was releasing anxiety over all that was being done. I was obedient to take part, and the Lord, in his goodness, was doing a work in both my husband and me.

Water from the Well

- What things make you laugh?
- How often do you allow yourself to go to that funny place and release those endorphins which will fill you up and oxygenate your mind and soul?
- Do you feel stagnant or alive with your life?
- Do you ever get outside your box and do something you might worry that you could fail at? Failure is not a bad thing; it helps refine and define our destination. Failure is only bad if we stay stuck in it.
- What holds you back from trying new things, as I did in the skit at church? It's ok if what you attempt falls short of the expectation put on yourself. Try. Accomplish. Learn. Grow and have fun while living outside your box. God never intended us to live with limitations nor a narrow lifestyle. Only doing one style of anything leads to stagnation. Find people who are different from you, if you are an accountant, befriend a musician, artists find a laborer. You can learn from each other. It's so valuable to do that consistently.

- Be reminded that Jesus fills our cup to overflowing when we are obedient to his still small voice, as he offers direction to something we should do.

THE FUTURE STOLEN

God is with me, even when death calls knocking at the door.

The phone rang, it was the hospital.
Me: "Hello."
"This is the hospital; is Brian your husband?"
"Yes, I replied."
"Can you come up to the hospital? There's been an accident."

My blood ran cold. My mind was reeling.

Just days, and weeks before, God moved in Brian's mind and heart after the Banquet Skit. One day he asked me out of the blue, "How often do you pray?" I looked at him quizzically, wondering what he was looking for in an answer, and why was he asking this. (Was it some kind of test?)

After a short pause, I said, "I don't keep count, but definitely every day."

He replied, "How often?"

Again, with a look of confusion, trying to answer appropriately, I responded with "Once, maybe twice, well, all the time, I suppose. Just depends on the day." Further explaining, "It depends on the situation and the needs presented at the moment."

"Why", I inquired, "do you ask?".

His reply was priceless and silenced me with a rush of surprise. He said, "I just wondered, because I pray at least an hour a day, most days longer. I pray while I am in traffic, for you, the boys, my family, and friends." His response took me aback. Who knew, I thought.

Silence became a friend at that moment. All I could think of was wow–as we nonchalantly went on our day. The conversation stayed with me, with eyebrows clustered together, trying to figure out where that thought was coming from. He didn't expound. But the Holy Spirit was doing something within my husband I didn't yet grasp.

Days went on, and because I did not see the execution of actual change, discouragement set in, like an unwelcomed guest. Many years and years of prayers offered to heaven, to help him overcome the struggle from within his heart, were relentless.

Life does that to our minds sometimes. At least it does mine. I'm certain it did for my husband. There's one step forward, towards a hopeful positive change, then, quite a few steps back. Who wouldn't be discouraged, right? Yet we can create a fresh beginning after any setback.

How?

By refreshing our mind with God's promises that he gives us in the Bible.

My hope had been, over the eighteen years together, that he would fully trust God to strengthen him, transform him, as He does with all of us when we trust our lives to Him.

Eighteen years of midnight conversations about the Christian walk, living through the deaths of our babies, and a host of other life encounters, I prayed for him and answered his many questions. I waited, and waited some more, I had reached my personal time limit.

This moment I yearned for finally transpired the first part of April. The boys were at school; I was home alone and still remembering the exact spot I stood when speaking to God, but with a humble heart, releasing this man to Him. The words were precise and to the point. *God, you need to reach him now. I am done trying.* I'm tired. Each time I sensed hope, it walked in the other direction. He's yours. You need to change him now!

The timing of this conversation was a breaking point. I shook my hands together and chose to let.it.go. This man of mine has asked questions. He has watched my life and knew I loved the Lord. He observed my reading the Bible, how I kept accountable to the church, with the kids, teaching them about Jesus' love and grace.

He woke me up, too many times, trying to gain information, of which he was desperate for solid answers to ease his curiosity and confusion. Spiritual topics that he struggled with, simply needing the answers to help him be at peace. My persistent question was, when would the change occur?

I was totally surrendered, no longer holding on to his searching and yearning for direction with God. God had to take care of him how he may. I wasn't trying anymore. My job was complete. Done. I walked into the rest of my day with a simple trust that my heart's desire would be answered.

God, I said, he's yours. I wiped my hands that gripped the situation far too long.

So much can be done when we aren't clinging on to threads, intertwined where we shouldn't be hanging onto, like a bell bottom pant tangled up in a bike chain. Learn to let God do what only he can do in each person. You think a girl would know that. All right, so I'm a lot slow sometimes. Grace!

Two weeks had gone by, it was a Wednesday night, the boys and I were at church for the children's midweek program, of which I was a leader and the boys were actively involved. We closed the night out, cleaned up, and were running a little later than normal this particular evening. When we got home the boys were still bouncing around, much too full of energy at nine thirty at night. I was tired and was looking forward to getting them to sleep, and crawling in bed, hoping to read and relax.

I opened the door; the lights were off, my husband was lying on the couch, awake and watching tv. This was uncharacteristic. The boys ran into the house with hops, skips, and jumps abounding, as boys do, with small hollers of *Hey Dad!* as I reminded them to go brush teeth, clean up and get ready for bed. It surprised me he was still awake, as he'd normally fall asleep before nine. He quietly

The Future Stolen

grunted a hello back to the boys, and oddly enough, he did not change channels. That wasn't so uncommon, but he was listening to Jan Crouch from TBN, with tears flowing, saying the sinner's prayer. She was explaining the sweet salvation of Jesus, which was for anyone who desired true freedom, and eternal life. It was her heart cry. She meant it and was sharing it that night via the cable channel. He listened to every word spoken.

To take this a step further, let me clarify, my husband did n.o.t. like TV preachers. But Jan had a heart for God. The whole purpose of her starting the tv station with her husband was to reach people who might not go to church or could not attend a congregation. In this case that was certainly my husband.

Rejected from his home church, because I didn't belong to that denomination, he felt bound by what he had learned in the past. The rules implemented made it impossible for him to attend church anywhere. The encouraging thing was, there was something safe as he listened to Jan that evening.

It was in those few nanoseconds, I realized what was transpiring before my eyes. So many thoughts from years ago ran through my mind, atypical occurrences happening before my eyes that evening; I was beaming with excitement for my husband that evening. My heart thumped as I recognized my prayer was being answered at that moment. Finally! I wanted to shout to the rooftops, jump up and down, run around the house at full speed, from the excitement in my mind. This was happening, for real, before my eyes. My husband was giving his heart to the Lord!

I could rest knowing he'd spend eternity with God, our babies and those we knew who had gone before us. In those brief seconds entering the house, taking off my shoes, with the mother's voice, echoing bedtime preparations to my children, I imagined the family I had yearned for all those years prior. Finally. This was a monumental moment that meant everything to me. Paramount significance and a positive, life-shifting moment; I was beyond thrilled.

As I rejoiced, I was talking to God, thinking through "my" plans and expressing these ideas to Him. I'd put the boys to bed, snug as a bug in a rug, with expectations they would go right to sleep, zero talking nor asking for water and nonsense I had no time for. I'd wait for the right moment to enter the front room and sit with my husband, having the bible handy, ready to help him walk into the freedom of life, his eternity being confirmed. I expected our Bible lesson to go into the wee hours of the morning, keeping him up as he had done so many times to me! (Ok, yeah, so, you wouldn't have had that thought too?)

Are you shaking your head yet? In those quick fleeting moments, *I planned how the next steps of our new and quaint life would take place.* Never inquiring how God wanted this moment to transpire. Oh, he chuckles at this girl's attempt to layout what needs to emerge. Yes, my ways…... when I understood, that God, with his infinite wisdom, knew and had the perfect plan in store, I had to unfold my hands. God has his ways to shut the door to this girls' ideas, as well meant as they were.

The Future Stolen

This night I heard God speak to me for the first time. It wasn't a voice per se. It was in my heart and mind, that he hastened within me. But it was real. Telling me he had this situation in hand. My job was to tend to the boys.

Ha! I thought!

I had the audacity to argue back with the Lord of Lords, indeed! Yes, I dared to go *there, replying* under my breath: I have waited eighteen years for *this* moment. I want to, I need to sit with him, answer questions, talk it through, to make sure he understood what just transpired.

God, in his patience, told me *no, I've got this.* It was then, inside myself, I threw a two-year-old tantrum fit. Yes, right there at the front door of my home, the entryway to our living room, all this going on inside of me, with God, transpired in a manner of maybe, thirty seconds.

It happened ever so quickly. I responded not so well. Epic fail, with a responding no — to God!!! Eeks, should He have struck me with lightening?!? Ha! This is where the King of Kings, spoke his Word very clearly, and said, *be still, and* know that *I am God. I've got this.*

Psalm 46:10 was a verse I am sure I had read, maybe even a few times, but never memorized it, yet it spoke to me that night. Little did I know it would become one of my life verses. When I get anxious, uncertain and unsettled, I remind myself to be still. God's got this, even when I don't understand it all. His promises are always true, and they are for certain, yes and amen.

When He spoke that Word into my heart, I stopped. Sighed. Shoulders down. Deflated, I ate a bit of humble pie.

Forever HOPE

How did I think I could do better than He? With a small amount of reluctance within me still, I knew He was right, but I wanted in on this. Desperate to pray with my man. To hear the words, Jesus is my Savior from voice to my heart. Detailed information to know how this transformation came to be.

Was he yearning for this life change that only God could offer? Did he listen to a talk show, or meet someone at work who may have talked to him about Jesus? These were the things I wanted to hear about.

But God. I had to wait and quiet myself and trust Him above my own desires. I listened. The boys got to bed; I spent a little extra time reading to them as they laid down. I had one ear out the bedroom door, expecting to hear my husband call to me, to sit with him, the Bible at hand. Yet it never happened. It disheartened me. I shouldn't have been. But I was. I longed for this juncture. Many tears that flowed over the years we spent together, expecting this time to come to fruition, it was such a precious moment that I so desired to be a part of.

I went to my bedroom, rather slowly, put on my pj's, brushed my teeth and crawled into bed. I thought he might just wait until I fell asleep, so he could wake me, like he'd done so many times before, to talk about what transpired this glorious evening.

Morning came, he got himself up and ready for work. Nothing was spoken about the prayer. The day went on, evening came and normal was the word of the day, as was the next. I was drawing to the point of total perplexity,

The Future Stolen

asking the when, how, and why's which rushed through my brain. This wasn't moving forward as I had imagined. I was asking God, who became so silent, especially after the moment we had on that Wednesday night's conversation. I expected that sweet discussion to continue on, as Brian was about to grow in Christ.

The days passed by, Sunday approached, I excitedly told my pastor what occurred the Wednesday before. An eventful night it was! He was overjoyed with the news, as all pastors are when the unsaved give their lives to Jesus. This gave me more inspirational hope for the future, as the next level would be to have a more open dialogue on the Bible. I desperately wanted to share with him, together as a couple.

Week one, turned into week two. We seemed to be living life as normal. Nothing transformed. My heart was deflating like a birthday balloon after a party.

A week and a half later, was our fifteenth anniversary. With nothing special planned to celebrate, as our schedule was always packed with baseball practice and games, church and jobs, like most families. Brian came home that night to suggest we go out to dinner. It surprised me he would propose this on a Thursday night because we had work the next day. This would keep him up way past his bedtime! I expressed how tired I was and preferred to stay home, suggesting that we wait until the weekend when we'd be more relaxed.

He prodded, requesting we go out that night. What a reversal this was. Since I was the one petitioning to go out together on a date, which we rarely did. We always had the kids wherever we went. That was an important detail to us, because we did life together as a family.

He persuaded me to go, so I halfheartedly agreed. I was unusually tired that night, yet in his persistence, it seemed important to him we go out for dinner.

Green light, go. We settled the kids in, then left on our date.

Once arrived, and menus handed to us, I was re-energized. There was some insistence within my spirit that made me give in. It was a nice casual dinner. As we drove home, I was content, still super tired. But fifteen years of an "Endless Love", we needed that little bit of time alone. I was relaxed, and happy to have enjoyed this simple evening.

Amazing how an hour or two can fill up the tank emotionally and mentally. No kids bouncing off the wall, gave us time to communicate, and we even shared a few moments of uninterrupted quiet time. It's the simple things!

Then, like resurrection weekend, Friday came. Spring was alive, not just in the weather, but in our soul. The day was beautiful. Something about that first real spring day with blue skies, and clouds that look like marshmallow fluff. Windows opened, and the sweet fragrance of grass and flowers ready to bloom rose high into the air. That was happening.

Feeling so alive and having a snap to my step which made me want to whip through the house and clean it up all spic and span. Oh, what a feeling! With a high energy level, I decided to go to the gym. Something that takes great effort on my part. Workouts are not my friend. But the gorgeous day gave me hope to work towards improving my health. With dinner completed, the boys ate and went to play dodge ball with friends in the cul-de-sac. Even Mike went out to play. Something he rarely did, as he wasn't much into sports, not even casually with friends.

It was getting to be close to seven p.m., normally Brian would have been home, grabbed one of the kids, as he did, rotating the boys each Friday to have a special alone time, as they'd run some errands, and get a candy or pop. Something I normally wouldn't let them have. It was their special treat time with Dad.

The plan I had was to get to the aerobics class before it began, but Brian was late. I did not understand why. We didn't have cell phones, so the minutes prolonged. I was getting more agitated that he had not yet arrived home.

Closing in at seven o'clock, the phone rang. The hospital asked if Brian was my husband, to which I responded yes. My mind momentarily confused why they'd be calling me, as I stared at the caller id. She expressed that there was an accident that my husband was involved in, could I come up to the hospital. I responded yes; I'd be there right away.

As I hung the phone up, my mind racing, like it had before when Bryan and Mark were born. In fact, more so. My brain wandered into the many scenarios that may have happened.

Being that the hospital was about twelve minutes from our house, I imagined the accident happened closer to

Forever **HOPE**

home. I wondered if I might see the wreckage on the way to the hospital, but I didn't.

I yelled for the kids, nine, ten and twelve, to come in, thinking what a twist this was in our day, as they played outside enjoying their time, using up energy they needed to disperse of on this seventy-something degree day.

Reluctant to come in at first, they somehow listened as I gave instructions to keep the door shut and stay inside until I got home. They were finally at the ages where we were leaving them alone for small increments of time, to see how trustworthy they were. Like all kids, they enjoyed being "home alone". They bounced inside the house, unknowing about the phone call, I wondered how much to tell them. I decided not to say anything, but I'd be back soon, and if they needed anything to go to our trusted neighbor.

I got into my car, with all that was within me, I spoke a quiet prayer to keep the kids protected as I drove to the hospital.

Once I turned off our street, I began to yell and argue with God. Holding the steering wheel so tight, my knuckles were white, then realized if anyone drove next to me, they could easily wonder why I was talking to myself. My back couldn't even stay relaxed against the seat, as I had pulled myself close to the steering wheel. I told God explicitly, no. NO! ***Not now***.

No God! I desperately requested, do not let this be happening. No! He's fine! As my mind raced in those brief fifteen minutes to the hospital, I remember being grateful I didn't have to travel further to get to this destination.

I don't think I could have done the drive if it were.

So much was running through my brain. What happened? Is the car totaled? What injuries did he have? I knew one thing was certain. I knew that he had died. No one told me so, as the hospital employees are instructed not to give that information before the body is identified.

I argued the rest of those long stretched out moments, that he could not die now. We have boys to raise; he needs to coach them in sports. He needs to celebrate the highlight of our lives, help in the teen years and all the other things we had to look forward to as parents.

He needed to be with me.

The boys needed their dad.

I once again begged God for nothing major to have happened.

I parked in the emergency lot. Walked up to what looked like the check in area, asking the woman sitting at the desk, if I was at the correct spot. Explaining someone had just called me, I gave her my name, as she quickly and sheepishly did not make eye contact, excused herself, confirming Brian's death without words expressed.

Those few minutes felt like forever until the white coats came out, a barrage of them coming towards me. The lead physician who was a few steps ahead of the nurses, pointed for me to walk over to a private room. As they escorted me towards a very stark room, they were making small talk, of which I drowned out with my very loud inner thoughts; my mind verifying Brian's death before they even spoke those dreaded words.

I silently continued to argue with God, uttering within the many voices blaring within my mind, this is *not happening*. Not now. Not for a hundred more years.

Closing the door, my mind continued to confirm to my heart, the resounding death of my husband. It was all much too surreal. To too. To. Too. Too much. The fore-runner doctor asked me to sit down, as he pointed to the seat, of which I did not want to oblige to his request. Reluctantly I sat, with great hesitation. I wanted him to man up and tell me to my face, not have me in a submissive position where I had to lean my neck back to look up at him, in this small ugly white sterile room.

My mind was still racing, then I became perturbed. Why am I doing this alone? Oh yeah, because they didn't tell me to bring anyone with.

I was hopeful, yet in denial, that this accident only left him, at best with a broken arm or leg. I hadn't thought of the car he drove or any of the smaller, unimportant details, and needed to know what happened. Not that they were prolonging the statement yet to be told, my mind and anxiety levels were heightened to the fullest degree. Someone say something and stop hesitating, please, I thought, even though I am sure the delay may have been thirty seconds to a minute at best.

In the cluster of my mind wanting to erase the day, I had to resist the urge to run for the first time in my life. My heart beating outside my chest, I was certain everyone heard the thrashing.

The Future Stolen

The doctor that stood in front of me, as compassionately as he was able, seemingly calculated, and much too factual, told me there had been an accident with my husband, which I had already been told.

He continued, sharing that specific details were not available, but what he got from the police description, someone hit him, and we are sorry to say, Brian did not make it. Freeze frame moment. Say it isn't so. No words could I express, as I absorbed them like a bumper car into a wall at the amusement park. Crash.

No! Make it go away, take it all back. Silence. My mind crowded with thoughts which I needed to work through, alone. By myself. Someone make these strangers leave the room because I don't know them. They don't care. Leave please, my mind demanded to them while I was unable to express words at the moment.

My head hung down, as I was trying to rationalize the unforgiving reality that I understood to be tangible. Facts of which I had been informed some forty minutes earlier when the call arrived at home, where life was normal. Desperately wanting to rewind to that morning, or even the afternoon. Brian was alive then. This can't happen. It's not supposed to be this way; he was too young to die, not even making it to his thirty-ninth birthday only one month later. My brain seemed as if it would burst with the rushing of thoughts that I desperately tried to push out. I wanted to oppress what had happen so desperately, as they all stood watching me, waiting for a response.

My mind considered how they did their jobs. What are they thinking when they have to express catastrophic events to the families in situations like this; do they understand the pain? Can they understand the nerves that want to jump out of the skin of people who come in, as they must deal with life changing circumstances? Or do they become callous to their jobs because it's their norm?

It didn't matter. Nothing mattered. I wanted them to leave. Never return. They are not my reality. All part of the denial.

Moments after that one-sided conversation was complete, the nurse asked if I came up to the hospital alone. What a stupid question. Yes, I replied, with a hint of indignation added to the short answer. What I wanted to say, was *'do you SEE anyone with me, or do you need a special pair of eyeglasses?'*. But I didn't. I kept myself calm and collected, despite the whirlwind flushing through my mind, which quickly became my first rational thought.

I was suddenly filled with dread when I realized I had to call my mother-in-law. Oh, God, no... I can't do that. She can't know. This will be more than she can handle. The heart pangs were more pronounced than they had the past hour. The same nurse, who seemed to interrogate me with questions I did not want to answer, asked if she could call anyone.

I'm sure I mumbled as my mind was trying to wrap around how to explain the situation to his mom. It would devastate her, as you might imagine. I reluctantly gave the nurse the phone number. But as soon as the nurse left the room, I immediately had a twinge of regret. A stranger cannot be the one to tell a mother, on the phone, that her son just died. I had to do the dreaded task myself.

Such an incredibly awkward feeling came over me, as I was about to say no, let me make the call. Within a few minutes, she came back in and said the voice mail answered, but she didn't leave a message. Phew, a huge sigh of relief came over me. I asked for access to a phone so I could contact her myself. Strangely enough, there were no phones in this little white prison cell, as it felt like such.

They were kind enough to bring a phone in and let me make the call. The most difficult thing I have ever had to do in my life. Nothing compares to the arduous one-sided conversation that took place moments after I dialed the number. Details I wish I could swipe from my memory and heart. The shock, the desperate cry of which only a mother can comprehend. A surreal awareness was breathing life into my soul. An out-of-body experience and the rejection of truth could not settle into my mind nor heart. Reality at the moment was not my friend. Life hurt, and it hurt ruthlessly. Somehow, I had to push through these taxing moments, so I could leave this forlorn place, never returning to it again.

The nurse asked if we had children. My attention raced to thoughts of them at home, unaware of what was about to become a drastic change to their lives. Frantically, my mind could hardly contain how their reactions would be when they learned of their dad's death. They would each take the news, in their own unique way. Would they be too shocked to react? Would they scream and become angry?

Time would tell. Nothing this monumental had ever happened to them before. They would find out soon enough; their lives would be radically change. Never again to hear their dad tell them how much he loved them; no more ball games coached; no more puns nor joking around, that's now in the past. How would we get through this?

The realization of them being alone hit me like a ton of bricks. Thoughts again tidal waved back and forth in my head. I didn't know how long I'd be at the hospital, clueless at the procedure and timetable. Do I go home to bring the children to the waiting room? Once my mind reeled around the many thoughts, I realized that was not an option. Quick decisions needed to be made. Frozen in time with no clue how to process this nor how to move forward; I needed to be with them. Nothing else mattered. I wondered what the procedure was with a deceased body. Did I have to sign papers? Do I view the body, now or later? It needed to be expedited… quickly, very quickly. I wanted to be at home, in my safe haven. I needed my normal again. The battle raged inside. Push. Pull. Whirlwind abounded. I wished for it to stop, yet it couldn't. This experience felt like falling down a hill at full speed with no way of stopping.

I just became a single mom. These thoughts all transpiring in a manner of moments, like a tornado swirling around inside my head, yet it felt like a forever storm that raged and wouldn't let go of my mind and soul that scurried out of control. But I had to stay in control. I wanted this to be a bad movie and not my reality. How could this be happening?

I felt closed in. I needed to leave that small sterile room with no life in it but my own. Someone needed to explain protocol. I had no indication of how to handle this process called death, and what to do with it.

When will someone come back to talk to me, I wondered? Details needed, now, not later. My mind was processing the critical and crucial checklist items to complete. How many more people did I have to talk to in the hospital and where were these people? I desperately wanted the checklist completed, so I could go home, to my space, back to my world and be with my children.

What did that mean? How would I live in this trap called death? The "what list" got longer as time went progressively slow. Time became still, so it seemed.

A nurse finally walked me down the hallway, thankfully not too far from the original room, to "view the body". To express I did not want to do this, is putting it mildly. This was like a scene from a scary comedy movie. I half expected Brian, in his very dry sick humor, to sit up and point at me and scream "GOTCHA!". To which my response would not have been pretty!

Somehow, this twisted humorous thought was a release from the stressors. It helped to release positive endorphins in that moment, even though the thought was only a nanosecond long. My mind simply needed this dream-like experience because I did not want to confront what was about to happen.

As the door was opened, it was dark and gray, his body laid still, quiet, cold and deliberate. It felt like a prison cell. No cover, nor sheet over his body to keep him warm, a sense of security was what I expected, anything would have helped. It was cold. At least I was very chilled.... to the core. The nerves played such a reactive part within me as the shock was setting in. I continued to wait for him to sit up and laugh as if he were playing a prank.

I couldn't touch him. I didn't want the last memory of him to be death, however that might feel. I needed to rely on the memories previously lived. The laughter, singing, talking, real life. As my mind was blank from overload, an uninvited chaplain walked in. I know she was doing her job, but she was not welcomed into *my space*. She didn't even ask if she could come in. I don't do strangers when I am in painful moments, let alone a developing situation like this, that needed to be processed, *my way*. She, to be fair, considerately asked if I were ok. Then made small talk, which was incredibly irritating.

This "small talk" was filling up the airwaves, with things she didn't need to know. It seemed so rude for her to invade my space in such a manner, even thought it was part of her job. I suppose it was more her demeanor that was bothersome.

How old is your husband, she asked? Do you have children? How many? Girls or Boys? Do you live close by? Blah blah blah. Get out of here, is what I wanted to shriek at her. But I didn't. The polite mode set in enough to get through the maddening little formalities.

She sent me over the edge soon after small talk ended, when she imposed the need to call someone to bring my children to see their dad at the hospital, and to do so immediately. She demanded someone bring my children to the hospital to view their father's body. Simply stated, I said 'no'. I did not agree with her.

She became indignant and quite upset with my response.

Never in my life, have I ever had something rise up from my feet up to my head in utter disgust and outrage. I looked at her, while my brain was yet again, playing games within. I momentarily wondered if they *should* see him lying there, on a cold steel slabbed table, at their ages. Who prepares for this, I thought?

What is the RIGHT thing to do? No! no!!! no! no!! a thousand times NO!!!! My rational mind was set. This is *not* going to transpire. My babies will not see their dad like this, flatlined on a steel table. I can hardly bear it, there's no way they can. Questions of why this is happening to us were swirling in and out of my head, as I listened to this crazy chaplain mandate that I must bring my children up to the hospital. Repeating myself, with a resounding no. Nothing else needed. **I.said.No.** She certainly needed no explanation from me. I refused. That was that.

She subtly suggested that I think about it for a few minutes, understanding the shock of it all; so when she returned, she'd take the phone number of who she could call to pick the boys up and bring them to the hospital, as an order to me. I got her drift, and I thought, she sure did not understand my final answer, which would not change.

I must have had the look of frustration and bewilderment written across my forehead, as the chaplain pushed her intentions onto me. The nerve of her rude self, thinking she knew what was best for my family. Not on my clock. She was not welcome in my circle, never. Buh-bye! She walked out the door. Leaving me alone, with my husband for the last time. Surreal. Strange. I was not prepared for what lay ahead. I needed composure and did not know how to find it.

My mind went back in time. I felt a morsel of normal, in the midst of a very abnormal situation. In those few moments with Brian, laying on the cold metal table, I realized that only two hours earlier, he was alive. Twenty-four hours earlier, we were on our way to dinner as we celebrated our last anniversary together. These memories pierced into my heart, they've become things of the past, no more celebrations. No dinners, no anniversaries, no time spent together, it's over. It's now all packed up in a case labeled memories. What an ugly reality. Yet there was something peaceful surrounding me.

God, I said silently, please make him sit up. Please make this a prankster joke. The laugh can be on me. I just want him alive. With me. With our boys. I want the white picket fence, which won't happen if you take him now.

Please God.

No.

He laid in stillness, but alive in the welcoming arms of Jesus.

I couldn't stay in the room any longer. I walked back down to the initial white room I first entered. Quiet. Lonely. Crazy. My mind tired of swirling around.

The Future Stolen

Concerns were segmenting into bullet points of lucid thoughts rushing in my mind. These points wrapped around and into my heart like darts entering, as it crushed through my soul when I thought of our sons. Thoughts of my in-laws who would soon arrive, I wondered how they were, as they drove to the hospital to view Brian as I had just done only a short time earlier.

I had to regroup and prepare some energy and focus for them. I couldn't think past that moment in time. Nor did I have a desire to summon up how to tell my family. I knew they'd be supportive, but the shock, I just couldn't deal with that yet. I had to process my mother- in-law's arrival first. Then I'd go home to my children and somehow muster up the strength to guide them through the grief we would come to know.

Yet, as the yearning to go home was desperate inside me, I did not want to walk into this new situation; a house that my husband would never enter again. No more normal. No more complete family. My thoughts went back to the nurse who asked about my children, I gave her the number of our sitter, whom she called. She must have explained the situation, because shortly after, with much comfort that filled my heart and mind, a familiar face, a trusted friend, our sitter's mom came walking up to greet me.

Surprised as I was to see her, she was the first person to arrive at the hospital; I was really glad to have a prayer warrior sister in Christ with me. She could help me ask the right questions and sort out the steps that would be drudgery to get through.

As much comfort as it was to have my friend with me, to my surprise, only minutes after she showed up, our pastor walked in. This was totally unexpected, since I knew in the back of my mind, I would speak with him the next day to begin funeral arrangements. Again, God was filling needs that I was unaware of. I felt as if I could breathe again. My heart was overflowing with so much gratitude to have people I trusted with me, and to help me walk through a process I was not prepared for.

While explaining what I had learned up to that point, my in-laws arrived. Emotions and tears flowed; the surreal life set in deeper; this was becoming more realistic. It wasn't going away, as much as I had prayed it would. There was no more bargaining with God to change the situation.

Then, at the most inappropriate and intrusive time, the chaplain walked in again. I am sure I must have given her a dagger look with my eyes, as if to convey, why are you here bothering me? She was rude as all get out. Again, placing a demand on me to have one-person present go pick up the children. A firm conviction rose, as she began to determinedly state, that *she* knew what was best, as they needed to see their father. She was casing me down with her stance, as if I would submit to her attitude that missed the target by ten miles, as she was doing her best to take charge of my life.

My Pastor looked at me, with a low voice, asking what this was concerning. I explained, as she was gaining steam out her ears like a tea pot ready to whistle. She was not a happy camper. No siree-bob. She wanted to bulldoze me into bringing my children in to view their dads' body. Placing a demand on me to change my mind from something I had already said no to. I know my children and what they can handle. That was not the way I wanted them to remember their dad, especially as children.

Once again grateful to have a strong presence in the room who knew our family, Pastor looked at me and asked me what my gut was telling me.

I looked at him, with a broken heart, knowing, within a short time, they'd become aware, at a much too young age, these loves of my life, hearts of my heart, would learn that their dad died. Trying my best to stay "in control", at least for a moment, I could fall apart later; I replied no, they need not view him lying on the table as he is.

He slowly looked back at the chaplain, calm and firmly stating that the children would not be coming up to the hospital. Oh, my goodness, was *she madder than a buzzard who lost its food!* She retorted as she turned on her heals, with a "you'll regret that decision, you *are* making a big mistake". How heartless and unprofessionally she approached this situation. Never taking into consideration our family and how well we know what decision best fits us.

I am content to say, this many years later, that was the correct decision. A mother knows.

Such a relief came over me, grateful to have had my pastor there, to help us make the best decision for our family. A man of God, and a friend who knew our family well enough to guide and protect. I knew that I could not reverse what my boys would see, if they entered that cold dark gray room. It's not something they needed to remember, especially at their ages. My pastor, who knew my children, agreed with me, as I conveyed my response. He wasn't just saying that to appease me. He knew us well enough to hear my words and understood my heart to help settle this uninvited conversation with the chaplain.

Phase two of this eventful day was about to take place, as the eleven o'clock hour approached, my children were about to find out about their dad's death.

No plan in place on how to explain what had happened earlier that night. How does one prepare a conversation like this to young children? My mind was settling into shock mode. Panic, I suppose. My heart was slightly palpitating. I did not want to step over into the threshold of this new habitation that was inevitable.

A God moment surrounded me, as I was grateful to have my dear friends walk through this event alongside me. I needed them to give me that gentle push, guiding me in the direction that I needed to take, rather than run in the opposite way.

Oh, how I wanted to run in the opposite direction, as a tornado swirled around my head, in search of understanding, and praying for an escape.

One set of friends came to the hospital to drive my car home, so it wouldn't sit in the lot, so I wouldn't drive home in the surreal state I was experiencing. I am so glad for a bond of real friends who had clarity to think of things that escaped my mind. This small, but huge gesture was a gift during this crisis. Something so simple, yet so meaningful, kept me from being distracted if I would have driven myself home. Our Pastor, and another friend gathered quietly at my house.

The tornado swirling around in my head, was trying to find simple and appropriate words to tell my young children what happened to their dad only hours earlier.

As we waited for our mutual friend, who had picked the boys up earlier that night, to arrive with them, we sat in discreet anticipation and prayer; I was mildly frantic, my heart palpitating so, that I was certain everyone could her it. In my mind, frantic to pull together the least dramatic words to express that their dad died. I did my best to prepare for the worst reaction but hoping for the calmest reaction, under the circumstances. I had no clue on the direction they would take as they walked in, with quizzical looks on their faces, wondering why, so close to midnight these people were sitting in our front room, watching them as they were asked to take a seat.

As they did, I was on the floor next to the chair they shared. Heart jumping out of my skin, not wanting to say the words I dreaded and never thought I ever had to say, came out as gently as I could. Articulating, that their dad was in an accident that night, and I just came from the hospital, something happened to daddy, and he passed away. They sat quietly, as I expressed as clearly as possible, that their dad died, and he wouldn't be with us any longer. Quietness was their response. I imagine the sense of their uncomfortableness with everyone staring at them, waiting for a reaction, was quite odd to each of them.

Forever **HOPE**

Time was so incredibly entangled that evening, I think it was only a few moments that had passed by, when one of the boys asked if they could sleep in my bed. They surprised me with the simple reaction. I say with a heart overflowing with love and some lioness pride. They like me, didn't react openly, with others in their presence.

They quietly processed what transpired as well as they could in their young minds. So, with ease, I said yes. The idea of us nesting together in one room, being close to them that night, was what this momma needed. They quietly left the living room, and snuggled up in our bed... perhaps, in their young minds, it was to sense the closeness of their dad, where he slept, only twenty-four hours earlier.

They don't recall those miniscule memories now, as I have asked them as adults why they made that choice, they have no reply. My heart still aches as I write these words, these many years later.

What I know, and needed so desperately that night, was for a quiet solitude to hold those precious babies of mine, as close as I could. Life had become so short, so fleeting. The world and everything in it became unimportant. Nothing mattered, but my four walls within my home. It was there, we were safe. Secure in Jesus. Everything else in the world could float away.

The morning after came slowly, as the sleepless night dragged on; my mind in planning mode who to call, what to say to each person, and as I understood it correctly, each person responded as I imagined they would. Creating checklists in my head of things to do the next day, lists I did not want to make, nor deal with. Pastor would guide me through the process of funeral arrangements once the funeral home was chosen. The dates, times, ebb and flow would fall into place. That was the easiest part of the whole checklist. Walking through the steps was emotional, as you could imagine. But the rest of the weekend became hectic and yet systematized in a crazy wild way. The days were all an out-of-body experience, of which I hope to never have to walk through ever again.

Even in the depths of this unwanted difficulty, I was strengthened, yet again, with the Word of God, and how much he loves me. With Him, we have overwhelming victory. There is nothing in life, nor death, nothing that can erase His amazing love. No force or power that our enemy pushes against us can harm us. God has us in his care, He is our protector and overseer of all things in life and in death. It is for certain, a blessed assurance, Jesus is ours.

Forever **HOPE**

Water from the Well

- Death is a part of life. Grief is real. The key is to identify and work through the pain, hurt and loss. It could also be an ended friendship, divorce, job security, or other circumstances where there is a separation, estrangement, empty places or opportunities.
- The key is to talk it out with a trusted friend, pastor or someone with the grace and caring to hear your heart. Moving forward is important, no matter how small the steps.
- Have you experienced a major loss?
- How did you overcome the pain that may have occurred?
- If you haven't, what can you do today to walk through that process, which is so critically important?
- Dr. Norman Wright, a grief counselor and author states, "If you find there's an emotional connection to some loss, then maybe you have not really processed it. Maybe it's still affecting your life in some way". Take the time to heal fully, it will change your life for the good.

- When someone you know becomes widowed, be there for them, as uncomfortable as it may be, what they endure is beyond words sometimes. Offer babysitting services, make dinner, invite them over, the alone time can be so cumbersome. Have a listening ear to whatever needs to be said, as meaningless or profound as it may seem. This is part of the process to new normalcy.

FACING GOLIATH

God comforts us when we go through difficult times and allows us the opportunity to deepen our compassion towards others living through situations that are challenging.

Walking into my home the night death knocked at my door, realizing nothing would be as it was, a new normal would set in, which twisted at my heart. It was as if an uninvited long-lost friend stood in the way. I questioned how I could raise three sons on my own. The why questions were plenteous.

God knew my heart and was with me in comfort like a wool sweater wrapped tightly around my soul, offering His warmth and security. Slow motion was what my body and mind were settling into, the night I went home, after viewing my husband's lifeless body, never to be able to "do life" with him again.

The days, months and years after Brian died, were busy. The demands of single parenting are not for the weak at heart, yet worth it all. Days it became trying at best, as Goliaths would come knocking at the door with problems and issues I had to deal with alone. Simple things for example: how to relate to growing young men, when all I know is how to be a female. Living through the process of puberty without hurting anyone! Big life guidance with boys becoming men, them learning to drive and guiding them into their adulthood. Homework that I had no clue how to help them with, and helping them to become the best person, in a balanced way. The sump pump flooding the basement. Maintaining cars and trying to find mechanics who won't cheat a "woman", thinking she knows nothing about cars. Finding the balance in life, was a daily life lesson, as a single mom. The only one who loved them as much as I did was no longer there to balance out the testosterone and share in the glitches that arise throughout life in general.

There's nothing like the influence of a devoted father, and a mother to create a solid foundation for children. I knew I didn't want to baby them, which would have enabled their life; that would have been so easy to do, but unhealthy. I could have been incredibly strict, to make sure they obeyed all rules to prevent them from getting into trouble; realistically, I knew that could backfire too; children can rebel if given too many rules and structure. Somehow, I needed to figure this out – on my own.

There were days I wanted crawl into a faraway hole and let them deal with themselves! But, being a responsible parent, I dealt with the bends and the curves, as best

I could. Losing my temper and being snarky happened (maybe too often). Yelling. Saying things, I shouldn't have. Sometimes being too tough, and probably other times not tough enough. Finding the balance on my own wasn't easy. Often times my patience was tested, it was unfair. But no one said life would be fair.

Missing Brian often crossed my mind; wishing he had been there to help me stabilize the teeter-totter when life was a whirlwind of demands.

It must have looked easy from the outside looking in, since numerous people remarked over the years, that they don't know how I did it. Working, I went back to school full time, stayed active in the church, attended every sporting event the boys had. One child in Special Ed, and some challenging situations with a few teachers along the way. I went to every open house and did my best to spread myself between the three boy's teacher meetings, along with the rest of life and its celebrations. It was non-stop.

I got tired. I cried sometimes at night in my pillow. We laughed, we sang, we prayed, we had fun. We just did it. How? By doing it blind, do it knowing, just go and do. One day at a time. Live. Breathe. Do the best you know how to do. Glad to say, we all survived without any catastrophic events, and are doing well today.

How DID I get through each circumstance? Having a solid set of trusted friends who would listen when I needed to vent. When I was unsure if I handled a situation correctly, I knew I could phone a friend. When simple, or complex problems occurred, I had people who offered sage advice, or simply listened.

The Rock: The amazing part of my life is that Christ has been my Rock. There was no choice but to lean into His grace and mercy; he sustained life so I could get through each day. He knew each situation that I went through, before it even happened. He was not surprised at the details of what transpired throughout each season, especially through each death. I could lean on Him for assurance and strength.

Firm foundation: Every day was a day spent in prayer and a bible in hand. Praising God and putting stakes firmly grounded in God's wisdom as my Father and the guidance he offered. Although the Goliaths in my personal life wanted to slay me, I had many elements that helped me understand how God was with me. For instance, He would remind me, through memories of my past, showing me how he had worked situations that happened previously, not to harm me, but to benefit me, and prepare me for future events.

Count the Blessings: Another key component that helped me walk through the grief, was to be grateful for the wonderful blessings along the way. A card in the mail, or flowers sent to encourage me, or someone treating me to lunch, a hug from a friend, even a simple call to say, "I'm thinking of ya today!". It offsets the pain and helps the healing process when people share life together.

Never alone: The desire I have for you to understand, is that we are never alone. God is always with us as he strengthens our life, even though tragedies occur.

God's Touch: There was not a day that I did not see God's hand in something he had done to prepare me for what I was going through. The list is long and would be a story in itself for another book.

Extended Family: A significant factor in our personal path, was the true family setting within our church. The bond of Christ is one that is deeper and stronger than life itself. To have over a hundred people in your circle that surrounds you during critical times is such a comfort. People that prayed, visited, and offered to help, with no strings attached, is and was, priceless.

Jesus is the Answer: The Blood of Jesus runs through our lives. We share, care and bind together in all intervals of life, through thick and thin. Nothing is sweeter than that common denominator of His love, which bonds us to be a close and caring extended family, not just when it's convenient, but every day.

Prayer changes things: These folks at my church are prayer warriors! They prayed, watched, observed for classic signs of grief or sadness to unfold, wrapping their hearts and care around us was evident during the following years after Brian died. God was faithful to place our family into this church, which was a safe haven, full of love, grace and caring. We were very blessed to have a good set of neighbors too, who cared and watched out for us. It never felt like people offered sympathy, it was the sense of togetherness. We were blessed beyond measure, and I praise God still today for how he took such intricate care of our family.

Strong Bonds: Roots grew deep through the ordeal of becoming a widow, strong friendships were created. I want to say how much I appreciate my dearest, walking-life-out-a-moment-at-a-time friends, who listened as I cried, as they lent an ear, while the healing process of this widow and single mom, took place. (Launa, Bobbie, Terry, thank you for your unwavering friendship, I am blessed beyond measure to have you in my life. I could not have walked through this season without your prayers and love, which was there on a daily basis, as was Pastor Dave and Pauline). Oh, the rewards are many as we collectively care for each other!

I am who God says I am: A very important point that sustained me through it all was the determination to stand on who God says I am. There was nothing, nor any situation that could destroy me. The enemy of the soul is real. He does his best to attack. But God tells us, when we are at our weakest, it is then He strengthens us, when we believe and stand firm in Him. The choice is to live life on your own merits, or dive into the Fathers very protective arms.

Family Dynamic stays in tact: There was a new inner circle with just the four of us, instead of five, or seven, had our babies lived. It was as if Brian and our baby boys were the outer circle, keeping us secure within, like angels. What a safety net it felt like. God in the Center, and we walked life out and lived the fullest we could, despite the whirling circumstances we had to get through.

Resilience: As a single parent, there are so many doubts and concerns we carry and wonder if the decisions made are correct or damaging. Kids are resilient, when the firm foundation of family is filled with love and Jesus.

Live Life: Life is to be lived; activities like school, sports, church functions, friends, pets, house detail, etc. We walked out the days after the funeral, one day at a time, learning what this new normal would be like. It was oddly different. Often times peculiar, but yet, it was a fresh foundation we were building as a family. It truly was a whirlwind of nonstop activities, but it was all good.

Dreams and Visions: Gods' continuous and astonishing presence was evident through the grief process. I had many dreams over the years after Brian died. Brian would show up and be silent. The dream would be in a familiar place, with just the two of us. The dream always shocked me because he was alive. Then I'd yell at him, because it felt like a cruel joke he had played, faking his death, hiding out somewhere, letting us think he had died. Then, in a flicker of a second in the dream, I'd turn my head and he'd be gone. Dream over, that quick.

Through these dreams, God was showing me that He was my Husband, and He was with me. It was like a hug wrapping around me tightly. What a sweet gift of His assurance and His love for me.

God, who is the husband to the widow, was present and shielding me in a most protective way. He also gave an amazing peace within my heart and mind. There was often a sense of calmness amid the grief. Surreal. But comforting.

Praise came from my heart and mouth, as I realized the many ways God answered prayers.

There's an interesting reflection that comes with death. We have a promise to see our loved one again, if they are living with Christ in their heart before they pass on.

God is so merciful; he catches the tears we cry.

When we love deep, we grieve deep. Love abounds and it never fails, the love we share is always in our heart and mind. The root of love runs deep.

This certainly isn't the end of my story. There was one more big blow that would come my way via death.

Liz was an empty nester, and I was almost arriving to that peaceful time. We were at a great place in life. The next generation would begin their families, we'd become grandparents, and continue to share in our joys together.

But one morning, Liz called me. I could hear pain and hesitation in her voice. Something was very wrong. My mind raced, my heart welled up inside, knowing something was amiss. My first thought was something terrible happened to her husband, or one of her girls. She began with the words, "I need you to pray, now!".

My heart nearly stopped at the urgency in the airwaves. What she began to say seemed to jumble all together, nothing made sense, and my mind was rejecting each sentence spoken. My insides were screaming "NO!!!"

She had received a call from her doctor, early that morning, stating she needed to come into the office immediately, and to bring her husband. Those are never good words to hear. She was on her way to discuss tests that were completed and gather the diagnosis; she placed the demand if you will, for me to pray fervently.

Fear slapped us all in the gut that morning.

I dreaded those long hours, as I waited to hear back from her. To say I despised those moments, would be an understatement.

The phone finally rang. The momentary hesitation of not wanting to answer, so I would not hear whatever was going to be said, felt like a long drawn out skid. I said hello, only to hear the ugliest of words come across the line: it is cancer.

Unbelief set in. Dread. Arguments within my mind refused to accept this nasty diagnosis. This could not be so. Liz was a healthy person. She never smoked, drank, always ate well, and did things she knew to do to be healthy.

To top it off, it was kidney cancer, which had metastasized to her femur; surgeries were needed immediately. Many of the details were jumbled to me, never hearing all the medical lingo spoken. I wrote down messy notes, so I could remember something from this traumatic moment in time. My mind kept saying this is not possible. It's not happening.

The doctors gave a grim span of time, as they often do. Due to the severity of how "bad" the cancer had spread, from a medical diagnosis, they said she would not live a year. But they didn't know Who we know, the God of healing.

We began digging into the Word, praying, and praying some more. Never ceasing in the belief, she would be a medical miracle. We were certain of this.

Two surgeries happened soon after that dreaded morning. Miracles had been placed before we even knew the diagnosis. That is how our God works, in mysterious ways.

Having had just moved, they "happened" to be near one of the best hospitals where some of her doctors who were among the best rated for kidney cancer practiced. That was no accident.

The fact that God had kept her physically safe before knowing the bone had deteriorated drastically, was no accident. She had just been on a vacation the week before where there was a lot of walking on unstable ground. God kept her strong.

Surgeries were completed, she healed, under the circumstances, better than anticipated. Another "God thing".

Months became years, as she fought the fight of faith. We stood on the Word of God. We believed. Yet, cancer is a relentless enemy. Four years after the diagnosis, she passed away.

This was by far, the most difficult of all my experiences. The love and honor we shared with each other is something that can't be replaced. The questions I asked of God were demanding and as relentless as the cancer itself. What was the resolve? God is sovereign. Unlike Brian, after Liz's death, I didn't have dreams. I never received confirmation nor answers to the why questions. But He knows. Comfort came from the perspective of which we know, she is in heaven, dancing on streets of gold is what I have to look forward to: eternity awaits and is guaranteed; we will be together again one day.

Life continues.

As I write this story, the evidence of my heart being in God's palm with the death of each baby, had its own heart ache. But God's grace and mercy flooded my heart every day. Joy was mine. Jesus was healing the grief. He offered life in abundance, freedom, love and joy that overflows. Jesus is and was my refuge, a strong tower which helped me be the head of the household. There was no fear, nor regret in my life. The choice was to believe in what scripture had taught me.

The death of a baby is so dynamically different than someone you have built a relationship with. There's more of a void. More memories to recollect upon. It's a different type of heartache. The differences between Brian's death, and Liz's death were just that as well. Brian died quickly, no pain, no suffering, vs. Liz who fought a combative fight to this enemy called cancer, passed over time, and with much pain in her body. So unfair. So incredibly wrong, for each situation.

A husband and wife have a unique bond, we are different as men and women but need each other in the dynamics of a marriage. But that of a close sister – a friend, is a deep connecting thread that no one can replace. To dig deeper, Liz and I, being like sisters, knew each other from the time we were nine. We grew up together, we went through the childhood growth which is a sweet and wonderful bond.

The similarities that bring the most personal heartbreak, are not having Liz and Brian in my life. No one else I meet will understand the experiences I lived through as a child, like the two of them did. The dynamics have changed in such a personal way, it could feel daunting. Sometimes my mind and heart go down that path. But I have to, instead of wandering down the path of sorrow, run to the path where the Son leads, so I can live in joy and peace.

This peace can be yours too, in the midst of whatever you are going through. Just ask the Holy Spirit to help you. It just needs to be from your heart, your words, to a loving Father. He can handle whatever you go through, since he already knows.

Ask him for peace. It is yours, accept this perfect gift from Him.

Facing Goliath

Water from the Well

- Cultivate life by praying, reading scripture and study God's word with other
- Believe in God, who is the Anchor that keeps us steady.
- His promises are yes and amen. Believe Him. Live in Faith, even the size of a mustard seed, which will produce greatness within your soul. This becomes a firm foundation that won't be shaken when the trials of life occur.
- Love always. Love deep. Let go of naysayers and negativity. Live life to the fullest. Don't take one moment for granted.

LIVING IN HOPE

Never let go of faith and hope. They are the anchor of who we are in Christ.

As we near the end of this book, there are snippets that I "hope" you caught along the way. Take a moment to reflect upon your life, and how you got through each scenario.

I write my story, because these were monumental occasions that I got through. Life has so many ups and downs, but these were just the big ones. Death. It hit hard, shaking the core of my life. When life altering conditions come in and rock our world, sometimes we ask God why. Afterall, if we are "good" people, we think we should live with blue skies and sunshine. That's not real life – ever. Difficulties will always come our way.

Ultimately, what was the purpose in these deaths?

Well, what I know is, gleaning from death and loss, it gave me a beautiful gift of strength from within. It was

Forever **HOPE**

not easy. I would never have chosen this path, but it is uniquely mine.

I learned to trust God and his comfort and how to trust Him more through the circumstances. I was willing to allow him to help me walk through the pain so as to welcome healing, wisdom and growth.

Do I still wonder what life would be like today if they were here with me? Sure do! It's ok to imagine, but we have to be very careful not to live or stay stuck in the past. What we had hoped would happen could create a stagnation which is not healthy.

Like a boat has an anchor to keep it positioned in a desired spot we need to do the same in our own lives.

How does this story of mine relate to your life? My hope is that you find encouragement to move forward when challenges arise. It is in life altering moments we choose to trust God to hold us up and take one step forward.

Purposefully placing God in the center, we can have the confidence that the wind in our sail won't flip our lives completely overboard. He will calm the stormy sea.

We gain power and strength in Christ to overcome obstacles; be it insecurity, the death of a loved one, job loss or bad relationships. There is no problem to big, that God cannot help us get through. Absolutely nothing. Here's what we can rely on, according to scriptures:

He redeemed us from the destructor (Satan).

> He gives us such wonderful love and tender mercies. Oh, how he satisfies us with his goodness, so we can fly with wings like eagles.
>
> His powerful righteousness judges against oppression. He gives us freedom instead of bondage. His mercy is with us always.
>
> That is where HOPE stems from. Hope that endures and strengthens through the deepest darkest moments in life. We will have struggles and pain, BUT we have the promise of peace that only God offers to us.

We have the choice: live in despair or live in the well-being that God's got everything under control. Choose life by way of the Comforter.

I know this to be true, this many years later. I reflect back to see how God's fingerprint was written and planned out for my life. Pivotal moments, like moving to the "Podunk town" that I did not like, was the crux of change for me.

Without that change, I may not have come to know the One True Savior, who was preparing me for the future when my personal faith journey began. Blessed to have found extended family and friendships that I wouldn't trade for anything, became a gift that kept on giving. These roots grew deeper so I would not waver when I would cross the deep waters of life, like my favorite tree, the weeping willow which is strong and adaptable, I learned to ride like the wind in each season. Sometimes getting tangled up, sometimes rising high into the sky, other times deenergized and hang onto the Branch, because it's all I could gather to do.

Wouldn't we all desire a life of smooth sailing? If there was a perfect world, we would have no pain. But we live in a broken world, therefore, suffering happens. How we respond is imperative: choose to be a victim or live courageously.

You might wonder how to grab hold of the courageous way of life. Let me list the way:

Through the lowest of valleys, experience Jesus.

> Difficulties can be so challenging and disheartening. There were rough waters that brought faucets of tears that flowed full force, often from exhaustion, other times utter dismay, yet he gave me energy to keep living fully.

But God.

He is Comforter through everything. He catches each tear.

> How does faith grow deep? By believing Hebrews chapter eleven tells us how.

Living In Hope

> The Anchor keeps us from floating away from the shore when the windy storms attempt to rock the boat so bad, it seems certain that everything will flip overboard. Many ask, "Why did or does the anchor break?". Questions often left unanswered. But by putting the situation into perspective, the anchor breaking will either build or break us; why not grow stronger by gleaning from the situation. God never lets us go too far into the "ocean" of despair that he loses his grip on our life. We must trust Him.

It not in my might I grew strong but leaning on God to be the guide and my strength. You can have the same experience.

Knowing that life is to learn and grow, in the good and bad times. Becoming unmovable by the battles that enter our life is a big factor. We need to, during these rocky times lean into God with all our might. Even if our might is simply a whispered 'okay', because our energy is zapped. If that is all the energy there is, then that is what we offer to God. He knows. He is faithful to hear and do for us what only He can do.

Suffering offers perseverance when we dig deep into our roots. Despair can run down and tangle the roots of our soul to thwart us from affecting a confident future.

That's why I am here, talking to you today! Do not be dismayed when the weight of the world falls on your back, as it did with me so many times. It's only for a moment, sometimes for short periods of time, other times for longer durations. Hold on!

Weather through the storm. Remind yourself you do not have to carry this weight, but trust God to take the load and you will come out polished like fine china.

How can we be confident in trusting God? Only through His word.

Oh, the Word of God gives us so many great examples of people who endured through situations that were less than positive.

God leads us just as he did the Israelites in the book of Exodus. It explains so we can comprehend in a deeper level as we relate to Jesus walking through his desert time. Satan tried to test him just like he does us. The correlation is that Jesus was sent to earth to be an example of what we would go through, proving we are never alone, because God is with us, as He was with Jesus.

That's what I love about the Bible. Each person we read about in scripture is a life lesson that we can relate to today. God knew what he was doing when he instructed these amazing words to be kept for us to hold dear to our hearts!

God stays with us in these times when we could easily wave the white flag or check out. But he reminds us that the Holy Spirit is with us no matter what we go through.

He brings us miracles and wonders to show us he is with us, like he did when I had the many dreams of Brian. I knew God was with me.

Remember too, we never stay in these desert places. We can walk out from that visitation place, swiftly, or sluggishly.

The timing depends on what we need to learn, and how long we may stay "stuck" in the condition.

The hope that lives in us, is that we are chosen and cherished by our Father. He never wanted us to live in the hard places, but because of choices Adam and Eve made in the Garden, (Genesis 1), sin happened. The enemy gained momentum to have his own kingdom, which is not heaven bound. The question asked many times, is why bad things happen to good people. Honestly, bad things happen to everyone. No one is exempt. We often do not know what others have endured in their life, because they either have moved on or hide in the sorrows.

The great promise though, is that Jesus's blood purifies us when we are believers in Him. The love he has will never die. He is patient when we lose our attitude. He will wait until we surrender and run to him.

Spend time alone journaling, praying, put on worship music, and listen for His promptings. He talks to us in many ways. Through our children, devotions, radio, other people, etc.…when God is trying to get your attention, you will hear similar comments repeated, sometimes in different significant ways, pay attention to those words.

One of my life verses came after Brian died. Isaiah 43:18, which showed me that God was about to do something new in me. That verse was relentless and ran after me for months and years after Brian died. I had to pay attention, I researched and wrote that into my heart and mind, knowing God was opening doors for me so I would not be stuck in the place of grief and loss. This became my life verse. Anytime a season in life has completed, it's time for something new to happen, accomplishing one level in life, leads into something fresh. Almost like beginning all over again. Why? To learn how to trust Him more.

Through it all, there is a rainbow at the other side, and joy comes in the morning.

Be relentless. Have no regrets. Giving up is not an option. Learn. Grow. Get back up and go. Do. Be. Feel the pain. Be resilient. Let go of doubt, fear, insecurity and shame.

We are victorious when we believe in God. Be transformed, because God is always bigger than what we live through.

What's the goal? To be a person of valor, and strength. We perfect our walk one day at a time until we meet Jesus face to face. I am stronger than I was, but not as strong as I am yet to become.

Be encouraged. You too can live life strong and courageous with Jesus.

Water from the Well

- Learn to know God for who he is: loving, caring, and full of mercy; he is not a demander nor a solemn headhunter.
- In the storms, when fear creeps into our lives, do not hold on to it, we have the power of HIS might to cast that fear right out.
- Know God deeply. Be anxious for nothing, especially in facing the giant storms–and in little storms.
- It is God's presence that gives us power to face today when we call on His Name.
- Deal with tomorrow – tomorrow, today has enough for you to deal with.
- I encourage you to experience his presence and his love. It is yours for the asking.

FINAL WORDS

*We don't have to live with heartache.
We trust God and know when we do, our heavenly
home awaits.*

We cannot stay down, no, nada, never. RISE UP. GO DO IT! If I can, so can you!

God provided ways, simple, sometimes small, but always right on time. I see how he used that time to teach me what it truly meant to seek first his kingdom and his righteousness.

Life is a cultivated walk, as we are open to God guiding us, when we lean into him, there is a peace and closeness that nothing nor anyone can replace. *It is not by might, nor by power but by His spirit we live and have our being.*

Tests of our faith will come. It is for certain. We can't live in disbelief, which is sin and against His will. Our confidence comes from the Bible. He turns mourning into dancing, sorrow into laughter. He steady's our unstable heart and mind. We can open our eyes and heart, to stop and smell the roses and the goodness he shows us in each moment.

Confidence comes from Him. That is why I live and breathe. That little girl in chapter one, walked up the prison like gray staircase, entering into a new life in Christ.

He used a sweet young girl, eager to share Jesus with me. This opened the door to new hope, unconditional love and the guarantee of eternal life for me, my two sons gone before me, Brian, Liz, Antonia, my parents and so many others. Blessed Assurance, that is what Jesus offers as his guarantee to all who believe Him.

When I quiet my mind and listen to God's Word, his overwhelming love abounds, like a huge bear hug, I know that I know, it's a fresh moment, a new day, everything's going to be okay. This is my forever hope for you.

Sometimes the journey to freedom comes down to being grateful. Having a heart that is full of the Father's love. Appreciating my life, even in the circumstances, gave me happiness in the gifts of my wonderful extended family. To Liz's daughters, I love you to the moon and back. I am blessed to have you in my life, you bring extra joy into my life.

In God's sweet and wonderful giftings, I finally found my happy place, and am blessed to share the gift of art through photography, watercolor, and mixed media, creating through the eyes of my heart, which is refreshing, and therapeutic.

Vision isn't always in the eye. The depth of the soul rises up when we live what we are called to do. It took me years to find that sweet spot. It's never too late to find what you are to do with your life. If you have not found the gift that you can share with the world, keep searching. Trial and error are often the key to find the best you. Shed what does not work effectively and run with what comes natural to you. You will find the greatest gift of yourself when that happens. No matter what you are going through today, never give up, hope is yours.

I share with you, what I have gleaned through some of the most devastating experiences I walked through. I refused to whither and give up, I move forward each day, with new hope that only comes from Christ within me. All the glory and accolade goes to Him.

As we end the book, I challenge you to let fear and doubt go. Release it. Don't live with that daunting mood too long. When tension builds up, release it right away. Breath. Laugh, run, whatever you need to do to not allow that to build up and hinder your mind. Be thankful for who you are. God made you unique before the creation of the world. Mediate on His goodness, he is the author of your life. Take time with family, less technology, play board games; outdoor walks, laugh.... laugh a lot, with each other, sing silly songs, and don't forget to dance – it does a body good! Hug those you love often!

Forever HOPE

The difficulties made me stronger. I am not the insecure fourth grader who didn't understand how much strength there was from within. I was never that poor little girl/woman that so many pitied and didn't see what God's done through me and in me throughout my lifetime.

I do have days that I miss my baby boys, husband, sister-friend. But I don't live at their graves. I live in who they were, and they all still live within me, they each blessed my life beyond words. The lessons offered through it all have been a priceless commodity in my life.

The pain and losses were certainly real as I walked through it. But the rainbow comes out on the other side of the storm. It's a beautifully painted picture of God's love. He shines in me and through me. His glory worked through the process of pain, as we learn through struggles, which help us to grow.

Be you. Live in the freedom that you have learned through all your experiences.

Final Words

Water from the Well

Let me end with this list of points.

- This is what I know for sure, God is real. Jesus is the One Savior.
- God has many names, find comfort in these names (short list below). Please refer back to them often, as a reminder of His Power within you, when you ask Him to live in your life.
  - God is Righteousness, He has made me clean.
  - God is Sanctifier, He has called me to be set apart, and not like the average person in the world.
  - God is Healer, He will heal my diseases.
  - God is Victorious, He defeated those who rise against me.
  - God is Shepherd, He leads me and guides me every day.
  - God is Provider, He supplies all my needs.
  - God is Peace, He gives me peace in all circumstances. I will not worry.
  - May the God of Hope live in you today.

- I pray that in this short testimony of my life, He's revealed to you in a strong way the gift of salvation, and a forever hope that even in the toughest days, it will get better as you seek God, as I did, to fill you up with his joy and love.
- You can do more than endure pain, you can live free, with joy and love, the Love of Christ is calling you. Receive him today.

FOREVER LIFE

I hope that something within these words inspired you to keep hope alive. To live a life that is strong and courageous. Lives can be changed for the better as God calls your heart to his.

I'm a small-town girl from Chicago, who came to understand God's goodness, even in the midst of difficulties that happened. I grew in hope, love and began to dream.

Obstacles will occur in life. Do not give up; Hold onto hope.

If you do not know Christ as your Savior, now is the time. A simple prayer, asking Jesus to forgive you of all sins, he is faithful to forgive and will not hold your past against you. Ask him to be your Savior. He now, is living within you.

Read the bible. There are free apps for the phone and online. I like the New King James Version; it is easy to understand. Attend a good church that teaches the WHOLE Bible. not just parts of it.

PRAYER OF SALVATION

*I*f you need to accept Jesus into your life, or you may have many years ago, and need to return into his arms, He is waiting for you. Nothing you have done can keep you from his perfect love. Please, say these words, from your heart:

"Lord, I am sorry for running from you. Forgive me for the things I have said or done wrong in my life. I want you to take the lead and live in my heart soul and mind. I accept you as Savior in my life. I love you Jesus, thank you for the forgiveness that sets me free."

You can now confidently know that you will be in heaven for eternity, with Jesus as your personal Savior. Without him, we cannot live to the fullness now, nor in Heaven. Jesus is the answer to our every need. Always and forever.

Find a home church to grow with, get a Bible and read it daily. Find some devotionals that help you to understand the Word of God. If you need any help with how to do this, please email me at donna.foreverhope@gmail.com, to help you in your Christian walk.

ABOUT THE AUTHOR

Donna is a professional photographer whose passion is composing images that inspire people.

Donna offers the gift of encouragement, hope, grace and love effectively through using humor, compassion and creativity. She works in various mixed media to inspire people to grow in confidence of who they are in Christ.

Donna attended Columbia College and has been an administrator at her local church and the director at a local shelter for homeless pregnant women. An active participant and previous leader with Proverbs 31 Ministry's online bible study as well as Grief Share. Donna enjoys leading study groups and helping people overcome obstacles to joyful living.

Over twenty years ago, **Donna's** husband passed away in a car accident, she had to lean on Christ to raise three young boys alone. Forever Hope, offers comfort and healing to those who have gone through major losses in life.

Donna's sons are now grown. She has a daughter-in-love and two "grand fur babies," for whom she enjoys dog sitting. She lives in the Chicago area with her sweet Shih-Tzu whom she loves more than her cup of coffee!

You can follow Donna at these locations:
www.wordsbydesign.org
www.dbpbd.com
Instagram: dbpbd
Pinterest: dbpbd
Facebook: ForeverHope
Twitter: dbpbd

CPSIA information can be obtained
at www.ICGtesting.com
Printed in the USA
FSHW021714150120
66120FS